I0825204

Praise for *The CodeBreaker Mindset*™

"*The CodeBreaker Mindset*™ is a compelling and practical framework for navigating complexity with clarity and courage. Chitra Nawbatt draws on her lived experience and deep network of leaders to illuminate the often-unspoken rules that shape success. Her insights are sharp, her guidance actionable, and her voice both wise and generous. This book is an essential read for anyone seeking to lead, adapt, and create value in a rapidly changing world."

—Sarah Friar, OpenAI, Chief Financial Officer, and Walmart, Board Member

"In *The CodeBreaker Mindset*™, Chitra Nawbatt engages some of the most innovative executives from across industries to uncover the skills that empower people to thrive amid rapidly accelerating change. These leaders share the rules they follow—and the ones they had to break—to achieve success, making this a compelling read for anyone ready to create their own bold plan of action."

—Thasunda Brown Duckett, TIAA, President and CEO;
Nike, Board Member; and NY Liberty, Investor

"In *The CodeBreaker Mindset*™, Chitra Nawbatt pulls back the curtain on what it truly takes to navigate the complexities of career and life. She shows us that while every journey has critical moments, it's how we respond that shapes our trajectory. This book offers clear, actionable frameworks to decode challenges in business and life, empowering readers to pivot and rise with confidence. Informed by her own path and the lived experiences of influential leaders across high-stakes global industries, this is an essential guide for anyone ready to take ownership of their career and life on their own terms."

—James D. White, The Honest Company, Chairman of the Board,
and Jamba Inc., former Chairman, President, and CEO

"*The CodeBreaker Mindset*™ challenges us to think boldly about how we grow, transform, and lead in times of disruption and continuous rapid change. Chitra Nawbatt taps into her distinguished journey accelerating innovation across multiple industries—and the wisdom gained from pioneering global leaders—to share how to break through barriers, get ahead of the competition, and win on your own terms. The CodeBreaker Mindset™ Equation reveals a powerful framework that shows individuals and organizations how to reinvent themselves to multiply their impact, push boundaries, and create extraordinary outcomes."

—Sanjiv Mehta, *L* Catterton India, Executive Chairman, and
Hindustan Unilever, former Chairman and CEO

"In *The CodeBreaker Mindset*™, Chitra Nawbatt starts with a core belief that it is possible for everyone and anyone to build an amazing and fulfilling life on their own terms, achieving their fullest potential. Her life experiences allow her to brilliantly position it as a guide and compass for navigating a confusing time where chaos is the norm, and the rules humanity has long lived by are in upheaval. It equips readers with the knowledge and street smarts, or 'codes,' to architect and accomplish their plan of action. By learning the tools discussed in the book, such as written and unwritten rules, pivots, serendipity, and informed intuition, readers can build the life and career they want. *The CodeBreaker Mindset*™ empowers people to understand the game, compete, and win in various aspects of life."

—VN "Tiger" Tyagarajan, Bain Capital, Senior Advisor; BCG, Senior Advisor; Jabil Inc., Board Member; Kantar, Board Member; and Genpact, former President and CEO

"We live in a world of enormous opportunity and unrelenting chaos. Aspiring leaders like mariners of old need a lode star and Chitra Nawbatt has provided one right in the nick of time. This book will resonate with leaders who want to turbocharge their organizations and inspire all around them to higher levels of achievement."

—Frank McKenna, C.M., TD Bank Group, Vice Chairman; former Ambassador of Canada to the United States; and former Premier of New Brunswick

"In *The CodeBreaker Mindset*™, Chitra Nawbatt uncovers the powerful truths about success that are rarely taught but universally needed. Drawing from her own journey and the unfiltered insights of top leaders across diverse, high-stakes global industries, she unpacks the written and unwritten rules of business, life, and organizational culture with precision and purpose. This book is a road map to navigating the unseen forces that influence business growth, innovation, and careers at any stage. It's essential reading for anyone committed to excelling in life, enterprise, and leadership."

—Thomas S. Caldwell, C.M., Caldwell Financial Ltd. & Urbana Corporation, Chairman

The CodeBreaker Mindset™

The CodeBreaker Mindset™

The Unwritten Rules for Success

CHITRA NAWBATT

Matt Holt Books
An Imprint of BenBella Books, Inc.
Dallas, TX

This book is designed to provide accurate and authoritative information about personal and professional development. Neither the author nor the publisher is engaged in rendering legal, accounting, or other professional services by publishing this book. If any such assistance is required, the services of qualified professionals should be sought. The author and publisher will not be responsible for any liability, loss, or risk incurred as a result of the use and application of any information contained in this book.

Matt Holt is an imprint of BenBella Books, Inc.
8080 N. Central Expressway
Suite 1700
Dallas, TX 75206
benbellabooks.com
Send feedback to feedback@benbellabooks.com

BenBella and *Matt Holt* are federally registered trademarks.

Printed in the United States of America
10 9 8 7 6 5 4 3 2 1

Library of Congress Control Number: 2025050842
ISBN 9781637748565 (hardcover)
ISBN 9781637748572 (electronic)

Editing by Greg Newton Brown
Copyediting by Shelby Harbour
Proofreading by Denise Pangia and Michael Fedison
Text design and composition by PerfecType, Nashville, TN
Cover design by Brigid Pearson and Chitra Nawbatt
Printed by Versa Press

To fathers and mothers

Contents

Part III: Victorious CodeBreaker

Introduction

Do you have dreams that linger in your mind? Goals birthed, either a long time ago or recently, that you fantasize about but hesitate to act on? Most of us do—whether it's attending that school of choice, landing a highly coveted job, or forging new relationships. What's holding you back?

Courage? Confidence? Freedom and agility—whether emotional, mental, or financial? Know-how? Permission? Do you know where to start? All the above? The requirements can seem daunting, given everything going on in life.

Many of us have these doubts and fears. We feel stuck and may not have the fortitude to try. Some try, work hard, and follow the rules, yet still don't make it.

Why?

Because they don't know how to play the game. Do you?

Life Is a Game

Life is structured like a game. I'm not referring to children's recreation. Nor do I mean "gaming" as a verb, as in to manipulate or be unfair or unscrupulous.

We exist in a paradigm of players, written and unwritten rules, moves and pivots, where outcomes are decided by using instinct and informed intuition, skill, strength, or luck.

Whether you realize it, or like it, most things are not as they appear to be. They fall into game structures. At the time of your birth, you entered the game. Family, school, work, and relationships each operate within specific games and codes.

Yet, we're not taught how to recognize or navigate them. To survive, much less thrive, through life and a career, knowing the rules is make or break.

The CodeBreaker Mindset™

I was one of these people. Unaware of the hidden multi-level and layered games and codes, naïve to the emotional intelligence and cues required to win. I had to learn the hard and painful way how to become a CodeBreaker.

That's why I wrote *The CodeBreaker Mindset*™—to share what I learned from my stretches, scars, and successes, from proficiently rising from the trenches to the heights of six-plus unique industries, with no insider connections or privilege, only strategy and persistence. And also to offer insights from the fifteen distinguished global leaders from various industries whom I researched and interviewed in-depth for *The CodeBreaker Mindset*™. These leaders, in order of appearance in the book, are Dr. Astro Teller (Alphabet, The Moonshot Factory, Co-Founder and Captain), Navin Chaddha (Mayfield Fund, Managing Partner), Kazembe Ajamu (5Tre The Blade, CEO and Father of Zendaya), Ken Ohashi (Brooks Brothers, CEO), Reshma Saujani (Girls Who Code and Moms First, Founder), Steve Kraus (Bessemer Venture Partners, Partner), Jon Korngold (Blackstone, Global Head of Blackstone Growth), Dr. David Thomas (Morehouse College, President), Bruce Cohen (Academy Award and Tony Award winner and Emmy-nominated Producer), BD Wong (Tony Award winner and Emmy-nominated Actor),

Mindy Grossman (Consello, Partner and Vice Chair; Fanatics, Board Member; former CEO of WW), Ndidi Okonkwo Nwuneli (ONE Campaign, President and CEO), Tory Burch (Tory Burch LLC, Founder, Executive Chairman, Chief Creative Officer), Michelle Peluso (Revlon, CEO, and Nike, Board Member), and Yannick Colaco (FanCode, Co-Founder, and former National Basketball Association [NBA], India, Managing Director). You will receive their wisdom in their own words that they shared with me in our respective interviews. These expressions are meant to inspire you not to succumb to the status quo, but to soar high to reach your dreams, to acquire the mindset and practical skills needed to break into spaces that you were previously locked out of and blocked from.

We go through life thinking everything and everyone is transparent, linear, and merit-driven. Believing information, access, relationships, knowledge, and resources are democratic is far from reality, especially given the haves and have-nots, insiders and outsiders, and gatekeepers who strive to keep us out.

The Codes

Every ecosystem—whether academic, corporate, political, or social—has rules. The way into exclusive circles isn't just about credentials; it's about knowing the real requirements. These codes, or collective rules, dictate how things get done. They manifest as educational, cultural, bureaucratic, structural, and professional systems, which you should understand if you want to get in or get ahead. The codes are the ways people communicate and connect.

Many of the codes that will make or break your success exist in the realm of unstated behavioral and cultural rules and nuances. The way into exclusive circles isn't just about credentials; it's about uncovering the real requirements. When you do, you'll realize over time that these, too, are not static. The next opportunity arises when you have tuned into the signals that inform you when the hard and soft requirements shift, so you can pivot your strategy into action accordingly.

When it comes to signals, they show up all the time, but many of us aren't aware or equipped to spot them. Signs and messages can come from your intuition and informed intuition, as well as serendipitous or fortuitous encounters.

Insiders

Some people, like the privileged elite, absorb these rules from birth. They grow up immersed, watching their parents maneuver power dynamics, learning by osmosis, and inheriting an intuitive understanding of how the game is played. They are insiders.

For example, if your mom or dad is a CEO of a Fortune 500 company or the president or prime minister of a country, from childhood, you were exposed to these worlds. You show up in the world with this frame of reference soaked into your pores, consciously and subconsciously.

Outsiders

Most of us are outsiders. We believe that merit alone will open doors. But knowing the written rules is only the tip of the iceberg. Succeeding, especially at the highest insular tiers of society, is about mastering the unwritten rules.

These written and unwritten rules form the codes that equip you with the knowledge and street smarts to orchestrate and accomplish your plan of action. You may wonder if there is a list of all the written and unwritten codes. Unfortunately, there isn't because the rules differ based on context and other factors, including geography, time period, age, gender, race, ethnicity, sexual orientation, culture, industry, function, socio-economic class, maturity of any dimension, etc. Learning, navigating, and leveraging both types of rules are critical to CodeBreaking.

Leader or Follower

Knowing the rules exist doesn't mean you have to follow them. CodeBreaking isn't about conformity—it's about strategy. It's about knowing when to play along, pivot, or defy the paradigms and expectations of others.

From birth, we're conditioned to stay in line, to comply with society's expectations and systems, to think small and be realistic. Becoming a CodeBreaker means rewiring your brain so you can override that subconscious voice telling you "No," "You can't do that," "You're not smart enough," or "You don't belong." Form a new empowering mindset to get in and play the game that until now, you've been excluded from.

Know and accept that many of these game structures are not fair. They require elevating how you think and act. Tune your mind into problem-solving mode, stay sharp, and don't settle for the status quo.

Do You Need a CodeBreaker Mindset?

Yes. The rules of life that governed our parents, grandparents, and forefathers are gone. We live in a world where chaos is the norm (see chapter 1), a never-before-seen era of permanent turmoil, where transparency and trust have evaporated. We live in fluidity, where most things are like water slipping through our hands.

If you don't know the full rules of the game, you are competing from a deficit with blind spots because you don't know all the requirements and invisible influences at play. You are occupying space, existing in the status quo. This affects your ability to be alert to opportunities, to persevere, and to prevail in any context. Without a CodeBreaker Mindset, you risk being irrelevant, outmaneuvered, and left behind.

The Game vs. The Player

If you are vying for something, but don't know all the rules and miss out on achieving it, you can create self-doubt, self-blame, and hamper your confidence. When you don't achieve, you may misperceive the situation and yourself, over-attributing the failure to your lack of self-belief and abilities. When in fact, the issue may have nothing to do with your own merits, but rather with other inputs in the game that are outside of your control and influence.

In that scenario, you may continue to think and operate ineffectively. The longer you continue to flounder and fail, the more your behavior reinforces your negative thoughts and actions. The compounding effect will derail, dim, and diminish you. You may be less inclined to take risks or perhaps stop taking them altogether. Your lack of confidence will hinder or cripple you, keep you subverted and stuck, and will negatively impact your career and life.

How you see yourself matters. See yourself as a victim, and you become one. See yourself as a champion and CodeBreaker, and you will become a force of nature, a conqueror of life's storms, manifesting from nothing.

You Have One Life

Each one of us is a creator, here to bring something into existence. For this to happen, we have to be a real contender in the game, which means knowing how to play to win. Many accept what people tell them and scoop up whatever crumbs fall from the table. Maybe they get lucky. Many likely end up with an average or mediocre life, or as Henry David Thoreau put it in *Life in the Woods*, leading "lives of quiet desperation."

Don't take no for an answer. Don't be defined by how others see you. You don't have to become a victim of your circumstances or be oppressed by others or a system that *claims* you're inferior.

I'm the outsider who learned to CodeBreak my way past gatekeepers and naysayers into intersections that were beyond my vision. Writing *The CodeBreaker Mindset*™ is one such example. If I can do it, so can you!

I'm not trying to glamorize what it takes to break through. For me, it involved trial by fire in terms of learning the written and unwritten rules, pivoting even when I didn't want to or know how to, and realizing the power and gifts that exist in informed intuition and serendipity. This is the framework and pattern recognition for professional judgment and decision-making in leadership, career, and life that played out for me repeatedly. Once I became consciously aware that this had evolved into an anchor structure for me, I had the epiphany to assemble these factors into The CodeBreaker Mindset™ Equation.

I wrote *The CodeBreaker Mindset™* to share this equation and decision-making compass. It's possible to build an amazing and fulfilling life on your terms, where you live to your fullest potential. Be whatever you aspire to be—not what someone else wants or thinks you should be.

Snatch inspiration and fuel from the heights of excellence of the fifteen global leaders I interviewed and discuss in this book, and my own multi-modal and multi-industry roller coaster life, captured in chapter 2. In the first part of *The CodeBreaker Mindset™*, we dissect "The Codes" and each element in The CodeBreaker Mindset™ Equation. We then progress to the second section on how to "Become A CodeBreaker," where we explore how "Information Is Power," how "The Status Quo Is Not Your Friend," and the value in "Creating Ecosystems and Network Effects." The final segment progresses to the next horizon of CodeBreaking in "Victorious CodeBreaker," where we will "Study the Outliers" and "Access the Force of Nature in You and Make It Happen" to power your competitive advantage.

Are you ready to get in the game? My hope is for you to move forward, not limited by headwinds or ceilings, especially artificial and fabricated ones that other people or structures try to place in your life. Embrace The CodeBreaker Mindset™ and accept that you can be this intentional and powerful.

The sooner you understand the game and playing field, the sooner you can start developing The CodeBreaker Mindset™ to chart and pursue your plan of action. To begin, let's understand the world in which we're learning to CodeBreak by examining the chaotic macro forces affecting our existence. Knowing what we're up against will equip us to be victorious CodeBreakers!

Let's go!

Chapter 1

Chaos Is the New Norm

> The only certainty is that nothing is certain.[1]
>
> —Pliny the Elder, first-century philosopher

We are in the age of the CodeBreaker. The rules humanity has long lived by, the written and the unwritten rules, are in upheaval. The only way to stay in the game is to see what's happening beneath the surface and improv the right response. When we're slammed from all sides, we can either buckle under the pressure or become forces of nature ourselves and power forward.

Brandi Carlile, a notable folk and country artist, sings about dancing in a hurricane. It evokes such a beautiful, if not slightly terrifying, vision. In the song, she cautions to only dance while standing in the eye, the one place we can ride out the storm amid the world's maelstrom, and hope to survive and thrive.

Some say there is no eye of the storm in today's world. But CodeBreakers use their knowledge and abilities to generate an inner climate of calm, an eye within the hurricane of life. Once the eye is created, it allows us to maneuver to higher ground. Unless we're born into privilege or get very lucky, only those who master the art of CodeBreaking will ultimately win.

This is not an exaggeration. Change is coming at us fast and furious, from all angles, at an unprecedented pace. The values, frameworks, standards, and assumptions of the past struggle to apply to the present.

How did we get to this point? When did it all change? Who's to blame?

It was a perfect storm of circumstances. Here are a few of the causes that society is experiencing:

- Rapid advances in technology and artificial intelligence (AI) are disrupting every aspect of our world.
- Global pandemics and health crises are ripping away any sense of normalcy and exposing our many vulnerabilities.
- Mental health crisis has people of all ages struggling or impaired in their ability to survive.
- Significant changes in how we relate to each other personally and professionally. For example, there are major shifts in how people view their relationship with work, and what employees want, need, and expect from stakeholders.
- Tug of war over where many countries and democracies are heading and the values they will uphold.
- Explosion of misinformation and disinformation is leading to widespread distrust and discord.
- Erosion and thinning of our communities are fraying the social ties and relationships that once held us together.
- Growing wealth disparity and fragmentation are causing resentment and division between the haves and have-nots.
- Burnout is on the rise as people's bandwidths are saturated and exhausted with life to date, relentless change, and trauma.

You're not imagining the acceleration of chaos. It's been cranked to the max for some time. For all these reasons and more, you're likely operating with reduced capacity and patience. There's less ability to process, replenish, and push ahead than even a few years ago. It's not just you who's struggling. It's *everyone.* All the people you know from your professional, personal, and social circles—and the people you are yet to meet—are stretched beyond limits.

Living in Chaos

Living in chaos isn't new.

We are a world of nations and communities, built on disruption and upheaval. Some of it is bad and some of it is good. Previously, the arc of discovery, human change, and breakthrough evolved on much slower timelines. Yet, the advances made by our forefathers toppled the status quo by drastically altering the playing field and the rules of the game. Humans have been facing the unexpected since the beginning of time and have been resilient and adaptable. Despite turmoil, we've always survived and gone on to create amazing innovations.

Think about the advances we've made over the last several centuries. The First Industrial Revolution, which spanned the eighteenth and nineteenth centuries, shifted many countries' agrarian economies to those based on mass production and capitalism as people flocked to cities to work in newly constructed factories. Then came the Second Industrial Revolution, bringing us electric power, cars, and telephones in time for the turn of the twentieth century. The next leap ushered in the Information Age, followed by our current era of technology and AI.

That brings us to where we are today, a time of no rules, constants, or predictability. This is the beginning of the CodeBreaker era. Finding your grounding is crucial in this new world of uncertainty and instability—one where all the rules we once depended on to shape our lives no longer apply. This is a most urgent assignment. While it is not easy, it is possible.

It's Time for a New Handbook

Not that long ago, people could follow relatively reliable formulas to yield their desired and expected results. For example, forty to sixty years ago, if you wanted to earn a comfortable middle-class living, you might choose to become an accountant, nurse, or manager, and you would likely have been successful. Today, attending and graduating from the best schools and even obtaining professional designations or multiple degrees no longer provide a linear, predictable, or guaranteed path. The tried and true rules for success are obsolete. Even the career best practices from ten years ago, and sometimes even more recent ones, are irrelevant.

It's not just that the job market has shifted. The handbook for living a successful life got thrown out the window. If you're not one of the lucky few born into or invited into the elite echelons of society, you'll be navigating the storm not just without a compass but also blindfolded and gagged.

In a world of never-ending change, weakened and evaporating relationships, unparalleled technological growth, and the compound effect of everything happening all at once, you and only you can take control of your destiny. No one will hand you a golden opportunity. It is up to you to figure out how to turn the knobs and work the levers of ability, expertise, relationships, influence, and power to get the results you want, dream about, and are yet to envision.

I'm not calling on you to be some kind of all-knowing wizard. I'm asking you to be smart and discerning, and to use the tools we'll learn in *The CodeBreaker Mindset*™ to build the life and career you want. One that's extraordinary. I'm calling on you to be a CodeBreaker. Living your life in a vortex of unmitigated chaos calls for nothing less.

Don't worry if that seems daunting right now; we'll get there together. First, it's essential to understand what's driving the chaos. It seems that functioning in the world is more complex than ever before, and you should know exactly what you're up against. Here is an exploration of the modern drivers of disorder and some insights about how they are impacting your day-to-day existence, well-being, career, and life trajectory.

The Five Agents of Chaos

Agent of Chaos 1: Technology and Artificial Intelligence (AI)

Technology and AI have driven a high velocity of change, and thus, competition. Since the mid-1970s, when the early Microsoft and Apple computers were first sold to consumers, through the present day, technology-led growth and digital transformation have penetrated and saturated most of the world. The explosion of AI, with increasing rates of business and consumer adoption, only exponentially accelerates the rapid speed of tech-enabled innovation.

All areas of life are permanently disrupted. Where there used to be constants, there are now only variables—and the variables are more dynamic than ever. Traditional structures and institutions designed to educate and equip populations to own and drive innovation (i.e., education, apprenticeships, fiscal and monetary policy, government, regulation, business, and economic structures) can't keep up with the high rate of change. The old frameworks of reference we've operated under are no longer relevant. In short, all bets are off.

The pace of innovation from technology and AI is dynamic, and both linear and nonlinear. Innovations arise every day. This spurs only more competition, more racing and chasing for the people, processes, systems, education, ideas, innovation, and life and business hacks that allow us to tread water and swim ahead. People with the most up-to-date technology and AI can get "there" faster.

Agent of Chaos 2: The Breakdown of Reliable Data

There is a significant gap and breakdown in independent, objective, factual sources of data and information. Given the five agents of chaos, it has become even harder for people to understand what is true, verifiable data, versus what is false, a perception, distortion, misrepresentation, or manipulation. We just don't know who and what to believe anymore. This keeps us cynical and somewhat in the dark.

Also, with technology and AI, there's been an exponential explosion of data, information, and content. It comes at us all the time in our analog and digital lives, especially through the many social media channels. Technology and AI are being used to adjust, alter, enhance, embellish, distort, and manipulate data, facts, images, voices, videos, everything. We're surrounded by illusions, distorted reality, and information being presented through agenda-driven sources.

Think about the simple filters on cameras and social media that amplify appearances and sounds. Media platforms are widely known to be used by people to show highly filtered aspects of their lives. Visual filters make images and videos look good. People post curated content with captions designed to drive a predetermined perception or self-serving agenda. No wonder we can no longer believe what we see, read, or hear. Even the blue check marks used on many social media platforms to signify vetted and trusted sources no longer mean that. Those blue check marks can be purchased. It is getting harder and harder to know what is independent, verifiable, and accurate data-driven information.

Agent of Chaos 3: Thinning and Transactional Relationships and Ecosystems

We've replaced strong neighborhoods, communities, and value-based relationships with paper-thin groups and networks that are mostly online.

In simpler times, our communities were robust and reliable due to factors like geographic and physical proximity and connectivity, as well as relatively more in-person linkages, and aligned societal, cultural, and values structures. Survival was dependent on having a village or neighborhood of people you could count on. Communities and cohorts, based on shared values, did a pretty good job of taking care of each other. People worked in and fueled the local economy, and built strong relationships with those they went to school with, worked with, and lived alongside.

Today, we've moved far away from this concept of deep community as online communication has usurped the place of in-person interactions. Technology and social media haven't connected us quite as well as their creators envisioned. It's difficult to find deep communities on social media and online. These platforms, whether LinkedIn, Instagram, TikTok, Meta (formerly known as Facebook), X (formerly known as Twitter), YouTube, text, WhatsApp, etc., can be thin, superficial, random, and very short-form in nature. This short-form style of communication increases the risk of misinterpretation. This exacerbates short-form attention spans. Short-form alliances and transactions are camouflaged as relationships.

Will these online acquaintances be there in your time of need? Social media vanity metrics may not translate to real-world sway. How many of them will buy a product or service from you? How many will give you an introduction that leads to life, education, or career opportunities? It's not that opportunities can't come from today's superficial relationships. They can, but they may be very random and rare in occurrence, effectiveness, and impact.

Agent of Chaos 4: Scarcity of Time, Energy, and Bandwidth

Less time, energy, and bandwidth for each other are causing human relationships to deteriorate. It's very challenging today to maintain strong, healthy, long-lasting relationships. Look at your life. Do you have an abundance of people with whom you have grown up, gone to college or university, done business, and maintained ties with for many years? Taking the United States as an example, research shows that 54 percent of adults have fewer than five close friends, 8 percent of adults have no close friends, and 38 percent of adults have five or more close friends.[2]

It's natural to lose touch with people as we branch out, grow, and evolve. Previously, we invested in and preserved the personal and professional relationships that mattered to us. In today's vortex of chaos, multiple factors cause the deterioration of those crucial relationships. These include a rise in physical and mental health problems that steal our focus or make it hard to show up; shortening attention spans; the onslaught of technology changing the way we live, work, and communicate; and the ability to block or unfollow people with the swipe of a finger. Today's cancel culture encourages us to end relationships with people we disagree with or for whom we don't have the bandwidth to deal with. This should be no surprise after years of steep polarization and division, and the fact that the continued deterioration of social skills has disabled us from resolving disagreements and conflicts.

Irrespective of the reasons for social and relationship deterioration, the impact is profound. We're all less stable and less able to be an available, decent family member, friend, colleague, employee, or leader. We simply have less time, energy, dexterity, and capability to invest in and sustain relationships.

The scarcity of time, energy, and bandwidth also significantly affects our ability to see, receive, digest, process, and act on the data, information, and signals we encounter every moment of each day. If our bandwidth is limited, we may miss that traffic and the ability to recognize the potential in people we meet. Or we may see it but be unable to partially or fully discern who or what is in front of us. We may lack the capability to calculate all the data and signals to make the appropriate observations and conclusions about what is happening and how to proceed.

Agent of Chaos 5: The Evaporation of Values and Trust

It's challenging to find alignment in values and trust with others. Today's world is charged with division and skepticism. Maybe you've noticed how on edge everyone seems? We're filled with tension and anxiety due to the political, economic, social, cultural, and ideological turbulence around us, as nations and global communities grapple with values and beliefs. We're cynical and suspicious of each other. Every day, we become more polarized. It can feel risky to speak our truth or express our perspective because there may be consequences—getting blocked, fired, unfriended, or canceled.

With so many of us short on patience, empathy, and mental and emotional dexterity, conditions are ripe for turbulence and conflict.

In this charged environment, trust is wearing thin. We can't count on trust to build the bridges and sense of loyalty it once did. We've replaced allegiance with a transactional framework in all elements of our ecosystem. Organizations and leaders are failing to incentivize the behaviors that would build and sustain trusting, enduring relationships and networks. Having to deal with the continuous change brought on by technology and AI—the first agent of chaos—doesn't help. As a result of these transactional behaviors and relationships, people who may have once been loyal employees are leaving their organizations sooner. Companies are more comfortable with laying off talented workers than ever before.

Opportunities for trust decrease exponentially with everything being temporary and transient. How can you build sustaining, trusting relationships when everyone is out for themselves? Self-survival is at its peak, and it is the focus at all costs.

CASE STUDY

Dr. Astro Teller, The Moonshot Factory (division of Alphabet), Co-Founder and Captain

Dr. Astro Teller is Co-Founder and Captain of The Moonshot Factory, a critical division of Alphabet (also known as Google). The Moonshot Factory has not only been the heart of innovation for Alphabet but has created some of the most planet-altering technological advancements. This includes Waymo (self-driving cars), Wing (autonomous delivery drone service), and Glass (wearable, hands-free computing device or smart glasses). Dr. Teller leads "a diverse group of inventors and entrepreneurs who build and launch technologies that aim to improve the lives of millions, even billions, of people. [Their] goal: 10x impact on the world's most intractable problems, not just 10% improvement."[3] Dr. Teller stresses that "the world is changing faster and faster, and the truth is that's going to continue. It is not only going to continue to be at a high pace, but the pace will continue to increase. It's a lot for almost everybody. That's scary for most of the world. Given that's true, I think the most important skill we all can have is being ferocious learners. It's the skill of adaptation itself, which is learning. What can each of us do as individuals and organizations to be good at learning new things, to be excited about at least some of the changes in the world? How can we choose to see some of these things as opportunities instead of problems?

"Because the changes are just going to keep coming and resisting them won't change the rate at which they're incoming. We can, instead of seeing it as a tsunami that's swamping us, see it as the wave we can surf."

Resisting Atrophy

Admittedly, this all sounds grim. Living in chaos is not easy. All these agents of chaos are dynamic, nonlinear, and have a multiplicative effect. They are working concurrently at varying levels of frequency, intensity, and velocity. This makes it challenging and fleeting to find stability in our personal and professional lives. It's unnerving, confusing, distracting, and ultimately, it can throw you off your game.

In the novel *Lullaby*, Chuck Palahniuk wrote:

> Old George Orwell got it backward. Big Brother isn't watching. He's singing and dancing. He's pulling rabbits out of a hat. Big Brother's busy holding your attention every moment you're awake. He's making sure you're always distracted. He's making sure you're fully absorbed. He's making sure your imagination withers. Until it's as useful as your appendix. He's making sure your attention is always filled. And this being fed, it's worse than being watched. With the world always filling you, no one has to worry about what's in your mind. With

> everyone's imagination atrophied, no one will ever be a threat to the world.[4]

All these agents of chaos can leave us overwhelmed, paralyzed, and unsure of how to effectively operate. The nonlinearity of technology and AI, the breakdown in trusted data sources, thinning relationships, scarcity of bandwidth, and evaporation of values have created a chaotic new norm. The effect of this on our holistic being, especially our mindset, may be atrophy.

This discussion is not to frighten or fill you with despair. This is not about fear. This is about being aware of what's happening, especially as it relates to that which we may not be able to explicitly see, touch, feel, calculate, and compound. The first step is awareness. The next step is to be prepared—to equip ourselves and our communities to survive, and more importantly, create a life that works for each one of us despite the new norm of chaos.

I am sharing this information as a reality check of what we are all facing. Other people aren't giving out this information because either they don't know, don't want you to know, or they choose not to know.

A form of suspension of disbelief is also at play here. When we suspend our disbelief, we allow ourselves to believe that something is true even though it seems impossible.[5] Many believe that despite the five agents of chaos we've discussed here, and any other agents of chaos that may exist, most things are as linear and straightforward as they were before. It's convenient and easier because the alternative is very difficult to accept, process, digest, and move forward with.

Many of us think we are in the game, and we aren't. We don't even know what the game truly is, and where and how it's being played. You have to understand the game to get in it and build an amazing and fulfilling life on your terms, so you can live your full potential and be what you aspire to be, not what someone else wants you to be or thinks you should be.

How did I learn all of this? I'm an outsider who learned to CodeBreak my way into places and positions that I didn't know about, that were not in my frame of reference, and where, frankly, I wasn't welcome. In some cases, I found myself at intersections that were beyond my dreams. If I can do it, so can you. When you unlock and access your power and the force of nature within you, all the chaos in the world, not to mention the many gatekeepers, won't be able to stop you.

While chaos feels powerful, unsettling, and scary, it doesn't have to bring only destruction. Chaos can also lead to creation, opportunity, and serendipity. The point is, we don't know what the future will bring except, of course, more chaos. However, if you can accept and embrace uncertainty as the only real constant, you can actually be free from fear and limitation. That is a critical step to becoming a CodeBreaker.

Competition in every dimension of life and business is at the highest level, and will only go faster and higher. The five agents of chaos will only intensify and multiply.

Despite all the chaos, there is hope! In the next chapters, we'll look at the fundamental elements that are at play, whether it's the written and unwritten rules, pivots, serendipity, or informed intuition. Each has a role along the journey. You may not be aware of these elements. Business textbooks don't address these topics. But they are alive and active in the world. After years of navigating and breaking codes, I want to shed light on these fundamentals. When you have this knowledge and combine it with drive and determination, you will triumph wonders!

CodeBreaker Heritage

I continue to surf the many waves of the agents of chaos. Through real-life, high-stakes trials and grit, I learned The CodeBreaker Mindset™. Without it, I would not be in the game, nor have access to the full scope of options, possibilities, and know-how to win. Even if you're the smartest, most talented person, you may not manifest or live your full potential, capabilities, and influence.

How do I know this? Let me share some of my journey.

Chapter 2

Chitra CodeBreaker

> Don't you know yet? It is your light that lights the world.[6]
>
> —Rumi, thirteenth-century poet

I had to figure out The CodeBreaker Mindset™ out of necessity, the hard way, through real-life trial and error, success, and disappointment. I defied significant odds and excelled at the heights of more than six highly competitive and disparate industries, including professional services, investment banking, television and media, consulting, venture capital, and technology. In addition, I have held a wide range of multi-disciplinary and multi-functional leadership and C-Suite roles. When people meet me, they scratch their heads because being multi-modal at the highest professional levels is quite unique.

I was born in Guyana, into a family of very humble beginnings, far from qualifying as insiders. In the same way that my professional and personal background can be perplexing to some (in terms of the substance defying the form), so is the history and culture of Guyana. While it is geographically located on the northeast coast of South America, it is substantively and culturally part of the Caribbean.

My family's beginnings were rooted in struggle and resilience, born out of the need to survive. In some ways, so were mine, resulting in me devising and learning CodeBreaking organically.

Indentured Servitude

My dad's grandfather, my great-grandfather, was an indentured servant in British Guiana (Guyana), which the British ruled for more than 135 years. Like many colonies at that time, it had slavery. When slavery was abolished in the Caribbean between 1834 and 1838, the British shifted the system to indentured servitude.[7] In this new construct, laborers had multi-year contracts—typically five—where they would work on plantations in return for housing, food, and medical attention. Sometimes, these contracts were longer than five years, and in some cases, would last the laborer's whole lifetime. Researchers and historians assessed this new model as a "new system of slavery."[8]

My great-grandfather, Nawbatt, officially earned his freedom around 1965, when he was in his seventies. My dad's father, my grandfather Sonny Nawbatt, received schooling up to the age of eight. He had to leave school to work and support his family. My dad, Summer Nawbatt, was the first male in the family to complete high school. I was fortunate to attend university and am a proud and grateful graduate of the University of Toronto (U of T).

Several years after my graduation, I had the names of these three men, "Nawbatt," etched in stone on campus to recognize and commemorate their struggle, endurance, and values. They and their forefathers would never have imagined their names would be written in stone at one of the greatest academic institutions in the world, in one of the greatest cities (Toronto) and countries (Canada) in the world. It's a symbol that anything is possible.

Education creates opportunity, but it isn't the only way to chase success. In the few pictures I've seen of my great-grandfather, the harshness of his life and survival carved deep edges on his weathered face. His eldest son, my grandfather, Sonny Nawbatt, had only a few years of schooling and spent the rest of his life working. Years later, he explained to my father, Summer Nawbatt, that his father had not known the value of education. How could he know? He had been an indentured servant and never stepped foot in a school himself. Yet my grandfather went on to achieve unprecedented success because of his ingenuity and natural mind for business. You could say CodeBreaking was in his blood, and he was a natural-born CodeBreaker.

Relatively speaking, I've achieved nowhere near that order of magnitude of success, given where Sonny started. Imagine if my grandfather had gone to university and business school; perhaps he would have been a billionaire entrepreneur.

Natural-Born CodeBreaker

My grandfather got his first job at eight years old, working as a bellman and porter in the hotels. As a young teenager, he found a position working as a junior deck hand on Navy ships, even sailing to Nova Scotia, Canada, in the 1930s. Sonny knew he had to settle down and marry. He returned to Guyana to start a family and sold basic necessities in a tiny market stall. He saved his earnings and pivoted to opening a general store, selling dry goods in the capital of Georgetown.

After having seven children, he pivoted again at the age of fifty-two, launching a manufacturing company. Where did he get the confidence, ingenuity, capital, and know-how to build a manufacturing company in his mid-life? How did he know to travel to Germany to source and buy the equipment, and then persuade the German engineers to travel to Guyana to build the plant? No one knows. What we do know is that, over time, Sonny Nawbatt was able to provide a comfortable living for his wife, children, and countless relatives who came to him for financial, educational, or general life support.

El Dorado

Being deeply patriotic, my grandfather believed in the proclamation of the sixteenth-century explorers calling Guyana "El Dorado," the land of gold.[9] He invested in Guyanese companies across different industries such as banking, consumer goods and retail, natural resources, and manufacturing. The CodeBreaker Mindset™ that he developed, both out of need and through the various permutations and combinations of his life experiences, empowered him to understand business and financial markets.

On one visit back to Guyana when I was twelve years old, my grandfather invited me to join him in a business meeting with one of the country's multi-million-dollar (even by global standards) industrial families. During the meeting, this family's patriarch belittled my grandfather, minimizing his life and business accomplishments. He told my grandfather his manufacturing business in Guyana was small, and that he needed to export and expand abroad. This man, surrounded by his sons and grandson, spoke to my grandfather aggressively and without respect.

I'll never forget how my grandfather handled himself. In a clear and calm voice, he said, "You can do as you like. Guyana is my beloved country, and I believe in her destiny. I'm committed to my path."

After, when Grandfather could see how upset I was by how that man had tried to diminish him, he said to me, "Child, you don't worry with that. You must always know how to conduct yourself." I didn't fully understand what he meant at the time, but as an adult, I do now. In retrospect, it was an early foundational learning about the written and unwritten rules of dealing with people, especially powerful businessmen.

He operated as a man who had confidence and was faithful to his principles. He was always going to be professional and not let anyone bully him or lure him off his path. He calibrated himself not to lose his cool, nor stoop to or engage in the other person's negativity. From Grandfather's perspective, and mine, what he had accomplished was spectacular for a boy who had been robbed of an education due to his family's need for basic survival under an oppressive British colonizer.

Sonny Nawbatt was a man of color who spent a good portion of his life, involuntarily, as a second-class citizen in a British colony and then, in an independent Guyana, suffered under a dictatorship with continuous civil unrest and violence. Grandfather did not let any of this define or limit him. He managed to rise above the agents of chaos of his time. He accomplished a remarkable magnitude of success in business and life, given that he was born to parents who were indentured servants. He was a provider and a builder. He had a strong conviction of duty and responsibility to his country, ecosystem, and community despite brutal circumstances.

Abundance Mindset Over Scarcity

My grandfather had to battle scarcity, even over basic necessities such as health, housing, food, education, safety, and love. It was a different time in the early 1900s, when many families didn't have the language or frameworks for parenting and love according to our present-day definitions of healthy family dynamics.

Surprisingly, Sonny, who was given nothing, rejected the scarcity modeled all around him and gave abundantly to others. I don't know where Sonny's generous heart and spirit came from. He raised his family with the same giving mentality and desire to be of service. My father then coded those values into me.

Summer Nawbatt gave all he could to others. He drilled into everyone the importance of education from an early age and throughout life. When my father was in hospice in the last days of his life, dying from leiomyosarcoma (one of the rarest forms of cancer), I told him, "Dad, be proud. Even though you did not get the chance to go to university, I did, and all my accomplishments are your accomplishments."

The Nawbatt name etched in stone at the University of Toronto attests to the values, honor, integrity, character, blood, pain, work ethic, and life of these three men. They survived, and in some ways, thrived, despite all the headwinds and battles, the full harshness of which only they know.

This is the legacy I come from. When our family has all come and gone from this world, their names may be forever etched in stone, and the power of their spirits lives on.

Becoming A CodeBreaker

Ralph Waldo Emerson famously wrote, "Every man is a quotation from all his ancestors,"[10] and no truer statement can be said of me. The fight and drive I inherited came from both nature and nurture. Reflecting on my forefathers' journeys and my own life, I see all the elements of The CodeBreaker Mindset™ Equation (see chapter 3) in motion. At the time, I did not know I was employing a formula, so to speak, to make it in industries and ecosystems that were designed to be inaccessible to me.

Coming from humble beginnings instilled in me a fighter's mentality. Like my grandfather, I had to bust through the obstacles before me. That "figure it out," "force of nature," and "make it happen" spirit runs through our family.

When we lived in Guyana, we lived solely on my father's salary. He had been a draftsman. He surveyed and drafted plans to build roads, many in the interior rainforests of the country. In Canada, he got hired as a draftsman, but as a man of color, it was hard for him to keep that job. At that time in Canada, racism was prominent. He went to work in a factory, and my mother started as a typist for the Bank of Nova Scotia.

Growing up in Toronto, it didn't take long for me to realize I was different from the other children. Toronto is a metropolis, but it wasn't as diverse as it is today. As a result, many of my grandfather's attributes began to arise in me as a youth.

Learning to Make My Way

Early on, I learned how important it was to stand up for myself. When I was in Grade 3 (age seven), my teacher recommended that I be moved to an English as a Second Language (ESL) class. To this day, I'm not sure why, as my native tongue is English; however, I may have pronounced certain words with the accent native to Guyana.

Intuitively, I knew I didn't belong in an ESL class. I complained to my parents, and my mom called the school and intervened to prevent it. I don't think I knew what intuition was at seven years old, but I am grateful that my gut sprang into action to save me at a critical juncture in my trajectory. Fast forward and the irony of this is that I went on to become a TV news anchor, reporting live nationally and internationally.

Charting my own path again, in fifth grade (age nine), I was tested in reading and literacy and scored at the level of a second-year university student. My teacher, Mr. Ellison, said to me, "You have a spark." I had no idea what he meant, but that day, I went home and told my parents what he had said. With the benefit of hindsight, I wish my mother and father had cultivated that natural gift in me, but in all fairness, my parents were not equipped to know. Many parents aren't. I don't blame my parents for what they didn't know. I just learned from an early age to make my way. If it's to be, it's up to me.

Intermediate Math to Advanced Math

I learned young to champion for myself. When it was time to move to high school, students got slotted into basic, intermediate, or advanced math. The teacher assigned me to intermediate math. Intuitively, I knew that wasn't right and went to the teacher to fight for myself. He eventually relinquished, and I was moved to advanced math. This is funny to me because I ended up acing math and accounting in high school, was a teaching assistant for

Grade 12 calculus, and went on to earn the Certified Public Accountant (CPA) designation.

High School Detention

I learned the hard way that not everyone likes you, nor likes it when you defend yourself.

I fell in love with math, which was the cause of a lot of heartache in my last year of high school. I took a World Issues class that had planned a field trip to a garbage landfill. The problem was that it conflicted with my math class, which I felt was too important to miss. My mom wrote a note getting me out of the trip, and I went to math instead. This angered the World Issues teacher when she found out, and the principal called my mom at work. The principal scared and overwhelmed my mom, who said she didn't remember writing the note. The result was a month of detention in the principal's office after school. Worse yet, this infraction prevented me from becoming valedictorian of my class.

This loss was difficult to accept. Even though I had worked so hard, it was an early dose of the world not always being fair. I paid a high price for one teacher's retribution, a teacher who had never been fond of me. These circumstances suggested a certain irrationality or nonlinearity of serendipity, and in this case serendipitous headwinds were storming and intercepting my advancement.

Adversity taught me resiliency and innovation. Hard lessons and disappointments train us how to pivot, hustle, and be scrappy. When you're hungry, you're motivated. These are the makings of a CodeBreaker—someone who sees beyond the rules and status quo, who wants more, believes they're capable of achieving more, and knows it's possible.

Leaders Who Make a Difference

These early experiences are evidence that I was cultivating The CodeBreaker Mindset™, and The CodeBreaker Mindset™ Equation was in action, without even knowing it. Written and unwritten rules were hitting me left and right. I was pivoting to twist through barriers. The invisible winds from sensing moments of intuition and unexpected serendipity were blowing me along.

Fast forward, the power of the equation showed up again when I was a C-Suite executive at Deutsche Bank but decided to leave finance and take the plunge into media. After starting my career at EY in Assurance and Advisory, with a Certified Public Accountant (CPA) designation, I pivoted into global financial services. This included excelling in various operator roles such as strategy, sales, risk management, finance, and Chief Operating Officer/Chief Administrative Officer (COO/CAO). I was also an intrapreneur in a large organization at Deutsche Bank, where I helped build a fintech business before fintech was recognized as a new and highly lucrative business category.

During my time in financial services, I was fortunate enough to attend Harvard Business School (HBS). The motto of the school is "leaders who make a difference." This awakened a leadership calling in me at the intersection of business and information: to empower people by providing them with accurate, actionable information. I felt inspired by the idea of informing audiences with data-driven information (see more on this in chapter 8, "Information is Power") to make better decisions about their careers, business growth, investments, and personal goals. An anchoring principle in my life is to serve others through information. That's the motivation behind writing *The CodeBreaker Mindset*™.

TV News Anchor and Reporter

I discovered as an early teen that I had a secret passion to tell stories and interview people. But being a first-generation university graduate, I did not know that it could be a career.

At Deutsche Bank, I was frequently asked to moderate business panel discussions, and many colleagues would say that I had a knack for being a news anchor because they felt I effectively understood complex business topics, could capture gems of wisdom from elite leaders, and translate all of that for broad audiences to grasp. The fact that colleagues continuously recognized my talent was serendipity and the universe prompting me to recognize these qualities in myself, and reawakened my passion for sharing information to empower people.

After much reflection, including deep discussions with some of my professors at HBS, I transitioned away from financial services and decided to pursue a career as a broadcast journalist. This nonlinear leap of faith was due primarily to reaching within the heart and soul of my being to hear my intuition and allow it to proclaim to the universe that I believed in myself and would go for it. The positive data I received from colleagues that I had media aptitude signaled this was a career and life pivot worth pursuing.

It was the hardest goal I've ever accomplished. Why? The majority of broadcast news anchors and reporters have to start on local TV in smaller city news markets, which are highly competitive. I was able to catapult directly to being a reporter and anchor on live television, in New York City (NYC), the number one media market in the United States, which is the number one media market in the world. God, the universe, and the kindness of strangers and acquaintances helped me accomplish this. As a result, I am fortunate to have worked for some of the world's most reputable global news organizations.

The population of people on air as reporters and anchors was and is a highly select group. This was even more so in business news, which was niche, where there were fewer than sixty people on air reporting live from NYC on credible news platforms, and an even smaller number reporting live from the New York Stock Exchange (NYSE) on Wall Street and the Nasdaq Stock Market (Nasdaq) in Times Square. I worked hard to figure out the written and unwritten rules, constantly pivoting both voluntarily and involuntarily, listening to informed intuition, and acting on serendipity to earn and succeed in one of these highly coveted positions.

Coming from consulting and financial services, I had no knowledge or network in the media and entertainment industry to know the rules and ropes required to break in and rise. Five people encouraged me to pursue this dream. Most thought I was making a big mistake with negative economic consequences. Very few believed I could make it happen.

Making It Happen

I told anyone who would listen about my passion to become a journalist. Strangers and acquaintances put me in touch with people who put me in touch with other people. Each person was a learning opportunity, sharing good and not-so-good knowledge, know-how, ideas, connections, and resources. Even the many who said "no" or didn't return my messages taught me to recover from the macro and micro moments of negativity and rejection and keep moving forward.

Step by step, I learned, swiveled, and stretched myself to do things I had never done before. For example, I had to put together a reel, which is a short montage of me in front of the camera doing news reports. Since I had no prior journalism education or experience, I mastered the art of being ready with the elevator pitch of why I would be a compelling news reporter and what unique value add I could offer. I forced myself to wear make-up and go into "doll mode," which was not my natural inclination, but part of the game for women on television. The power hierarchy in media and entertainment is very complex and much of it runs on unwritten codes; navigating that terrain was a tough and scarring learning curve.

Relative strangers and acquaintances in journalism became industry mentors. Technical operators and behind-the-scenes engineers taught me camera shots and angles, audio, and lighting. I invested in a media coach. Retired news reporters and producers taught me how to write and tell stories for television. Uncovering and gaining knowledge from these sources was part of the unwritten rules to learn. Being relevant and resonating with audiences was critical, as storytelling in each part of the globe is diverse and nuanced. I studied content creation for different parts of the world because I had global audiences and did live shows customized for regions such as North America, South America, Europe, Asia, Africa, and Australia. My passion and determination fueled my insatiable hunger to achieve excellence in my craft.

I made it happen.

When I reflect and analyze the forward, backward, and sideways outcomes in the journeys of my forefathers and me that are shared in these pages, they are the individual and aggregate results from implementing The CodeBreaker Mindset™ Equation and The CodeBreaker Mindset™.

Are you ready to make it happen? Let's dive into The CodeBreaker Mindset™ Equation next to reveal the positive possibilities.

PART I

The Codes

Chapter 3

The CodeBreaker Mindset™ Equation

> I'm a student of patterns. At heart, I'm a physicist. I look at everything in my life as trying to find the single equation, the theory of everything.[11]
>
> —Will Smith, Academy Award–winning and Emmy-nominated Actor

Any goal or dream, whether it is education, career, relationships, knowledge, resources, wealth, experience, etc., involves a game of sorts. That game includes a series of written and unwritten rules and requirements. Binary and non-binary. Tangible and intangible. Fixed and evolving.

Ask yourself, *Am I in the game? Do I know what the game is? Do I know the written and unwritten rules? Am I informed and equipped to be a contender?*

What elements do you need to prepare yourself to compete? Once the components are fully assembled, it's time to determine the best order in which to execute them so you can achieve optimal outcomes. I call these stitched-together elements The CodeBreaker Mindset™ Equation, or for technical types, The CodeBreaker Mindset™ Algorithm. At a time when chaos is at every turn, having a succinct model that incorporates all the necessary ingredients to find success is an effective way to move toward your goals.

Here's something that may shock you: This equation has been dancing in your life from the very beginning. Since the dawn of time, people have been interacting using written and unwritten rules, responding with pivots or variations in actions, capitalizing on serendipitous moments, and using informed intuition to draw conclusions and determine the next best action.

Just because we weren't formally taught this equation in school does not mean it's not alive and well and active everywhere from Main Street to Wall Street. This isn't privileged information only available to those in Ivy League schools or top-tier income earners. You don't need those credentials to put this equation to good use.

The other essential aspect of this is understanding that the written, and more importantly, unwritten, rules help you grasp the game. We often think we are in the game, but we're not. Just because you get a job at a key employer of choice does not give you the knowledge of the inner workings and how to ascend and succeed in that organization or industry. You must distinguish between admission, getting in the door, staying, and moving into a position of being a real player or contestant in that intersection.

I once had a colleague who was vying for a job as an assistant to a big Hollywood agent. The agent asked him to prepare some analysis and requested it on a certain date; let's say, for example, May 1. The colleague submitted the analysis requested at 12:01 AM on May 1, while those he was challenging provided their entry by 5 PM on May 1. That early submission set my colleague apart in a competitive field, and ultimately, he secured the job.

The written and unwritten rules, as well as the other elements in The CodeBreaker Mindset™ Equation—pivots, serendipity, and informed intuition—help you understand what game you're playing, the binary and non-binary nuances, and how to compete and win. This is the purpose of The CodeBreaker Mindset™, a guide and compass for a confusing time where chaos is the norm.

Not a Math Person?

Before I share the equation, you may be feeling intimidated, thinking, *Hey, I'm not a math person*. Don't be concerned. We will take it slow and drill deep into each of these elements in the coming chapters. But remember, the equation is simply a way to communicate a reality that's already happening to everyone and has been happening since the dawn of time!

Learning these explicit skills will boost your decision-making abilities and elevate your chances of securing whatever goal you've set your sights on. If you want an edge, then harness this information to work for you, especially because most things in life are not as they appear. There is very little you can see, read, and consume that can be taken at face value, whether in books, narratives, news, social media, career, or life.

This is your opportunity to get in the driver's seat, take back control of your life, and subdue the forces working against you. You will be equipped to think, act, and navigate differently. You will be a proactive participant, not defensive or reactive when the unexpected or inertia sneaks in. You'll be operating from a place of self-empowerment.

The CodeBreaker Mindset™ Equation

[(Written Rules + Unwritten Rules) × Pivots] $^{\text{Serendipity, Informed Intuition}}$ **=**

Professional Judgment and Decision

The CodeBreaker Mindset™ Equation is a combination of the following elements:

- Learning the written and unwritten rules
- Executing pivots, both voluntary and involuntary
- Being aware of and acting on serendipitous moments, which can be linear or nonlinear tailwinds and headwinds
- Using informed intuition as a guide

When you combine these elements, you're able to make sound professional judgments and decisions, giving you the CodeBreaker, or insider's, advantage. We'll get comfortable with each element of the equation and show the power that comes from linking them together. In the game of life, unfortunately, it isn't merit that gets rewarded, but mediocrity. Mediocrity rises faster than excellence.

When I worked in global investment banking at Deutsche Bank, I had a senior colleague, Dan, who told me, "Chitra, there are A players, B players, and C players. Not everyone likes the A players. For the B and C players, you have to learn how to get productivity out of them, slow down, and go at their pace."

I exclaimed, "So, being average and mediocre are tolerated, and rise faster than excellence? Wow, merit does not take the day!" My balloon was popped. Everything I'd been taught about work ethic as a child and in university was shattered.

Now, I want to flag something. If being an A, B, or C player is the best of your capability, then by all means, let's acknowledge that. Not everyone is an A player, nor strives to be, and that is okay. Nothing wrong with that. The issue is when the B or C player is recognized and treated as though they are the A player, and the A player is told to take a back seat or is not given their just rewards. This often happens in the workplace. Are you wondering why?

Recall a time when you were really good at something. You may have had people around you who cheered your talents and strengths, and maybe some who didn't. In the workplace, for example, you may have had colleagues, bosses, or subordinates who were not as good as you, and they tried to thwart you by playing politics, downplaying your performance, or finding fault with your work. They were relatively insecure and had a scarcity mindset.

Going back to the agents of chaos, fear, insecurity, and scarcity mindset, they are being fueled even more. It's human nature to be jealous of others, or feel deficient, or not want others to get ahead. We may not be able to assess ourselves as that B or C player accurately; we don't want to admit it to ourselves. So we pull down other people, especially the A players. We want to get ahead however we can, so if it's playing the politics and favoritism game, and not merit, all the better. This fuels B and C players engaging in political treachery and trickery, and whatever other means it takes to rise. That's how mediocrity rises faster than excellence. Note, I am not saying that A players don't engage in political treachery and trickery too. Everyone has this potential.

There's a parallel here in math with normal distribution, popularly known as the Bell Curve.[12]

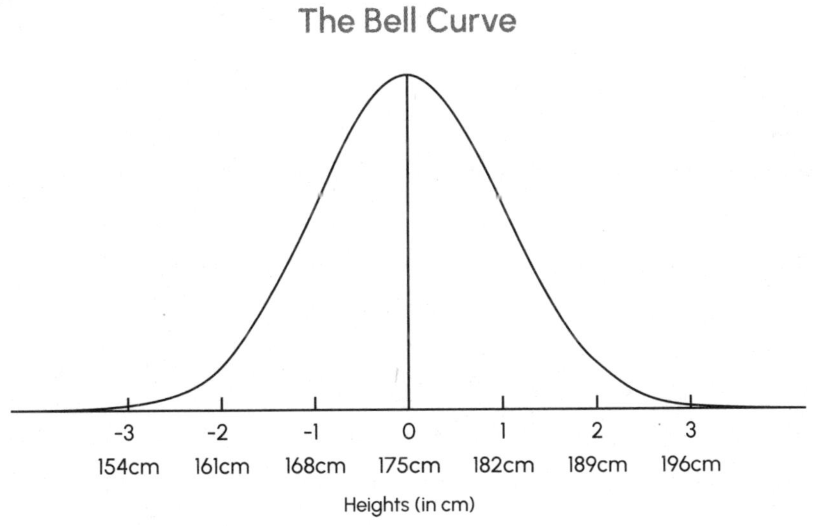

This picture may look familiar to you. Many of us all over the world learned this in school, especially when teachers would tell us how they graded the class based on a curve. Using school grades as an example, the majority of students were in the middle, or average. A small number of students did poorly (the left tail). Very few students did well (the right tail). When we take the median score of students, it's not those earning A's that benefit from applying this curve, but the ones who are in the middle, scoring B's and C's. When the lowest common denominator wins, something in the success formula is broken. There are a few A players, a lot of B players, and some C players. So mediocrity or anything less than excellence rises the fastest.

In 2024, a Pew Research report found that 54 percent of Americans get their news from social media.[13] "Users say they regularly encounter false and misleading content on social media."[14] According to Science Advances, "In recent years, the propagation of misinformation on social media has been a major focus of attention. Worries about 'fake news,' related to both politics and health [. . .], have led many to see social media as a threat to modern societies (and not, for example, as a tool for promoting collective intelligence and action). Common to such critiques is the assertion that people are more likely to fall for fake news on social media relative to other sources."[15]

If a high proportion of people rely on social media for news and it interferes with and hampers truth discernment, then they are relying on information with a high degree of risk, error, and distortion; thus, they are making decisions with a high degree of risk and error. This is yet another example of a population's average base of knowledge being pulled down to mediocrity. It's time to move beyond sound bites. The CodeBreaker Mindset™ Equation presents a new way to achieve discernment that is data-driven.

The notion that mediocrity rises faster than excellence is also a part of the game. Take a moment to reflect on your life experiences—whether from school, extracurricular activities, or your career. Did the best performer, from a merit perspective, always win or get their just rewards? Or were people put in favorable positions because of any factor other than merit? This is the game of life and how things work. This is what makes The CodeBreaker Mindset™ Equation necessary. Decode what is going on in a situation. Ask yourself, *What should be going on?* Knowing the formula of written and unwritten rules, pivots, serendipity, and informed intuition will help you jockey around mediocrity, bad averages, and headwinds that interfere with merit-driven outcomes and excellence.

In the next few chapters, we'll break down the written and unwritten rules, explore the pivots, and look at how serendipity and informed intuition interact to position you with a competitive edge.

Chapter 4

Written and Unwritten Rules

> Learn the rules like a pro, so you can break them like an artist.[16]
>
> —Pablo Picasso, renowned painter, sculptor, and co-founder of Cubism

The written and unwritten rules are the starting elements of The Code-Breaker Mindset™ Equation. To acquire what we're pursuing, we either need to follow the rules or, as is sometimes the case, massage, adjust, or override them altogether. Whether you decide to adhere to the rules or be a renegade and shatter them into a million pieces, you first need to know what they are.

The Written Rules

The CodeBreaker Mindset™ Equation

[(**Written Rules** + Unwritten Rules) × Pivots] $^{\text{Serendipity, Informed Intuition}}$ =

Professional Judgment and Decision

The first element of The CodeBreaker Mindset™ Equation is written rules, which are prescriptive requirements that everyone usually has to follow. They are the collective rules for how things are done. They manifest as cultural, bureaucratic, structural, and professional systems, which are essential to understand if you want to get in or get ahead. The codes are the ways people communicate and connect. For example, to qualify to be a professionally licensed doctor, lawyer, or accountant, a person needs to fulfill curricula and courses, achieve certain grades, pass examinations, complete hours of training and work, etc. These minimum requirements provide a clear starting point.

Within written rules, there are levels and layers. Not all written rules are made fully accessible to the public, or they aren't communicated in a way that everyone can understand. They may be encrypted. Some codes aren't in plain sight and need to be hunted down. This means checking multiple sources, asking those involved directly and adjacent, cross-referencing data, and analyzing the information presented. Then, ask yourself, *Have I identified and retrieved all the written rules?*

For example, when I was applying to the U of T to do my undergraduate degree, there were a series of admission requirements. Most, if not all, colleges and universities have minimum admission requirements that include academic, leadership, and extracurricular components. At U of T, this included completing high school with a certain grade point average and requisite credits. In the application, I also had to write about my goals, leadership experience, and extracurricular activities. The form had to be submitted in a certain format, with the fees paid by a deadline. There was guidance in the admission package on how to fulfill all these requirements, but there was still a lot of ambiguity. While I was an A+ student and had a strong application package, was it enough? How could I know with certainty what U of T's cut-off thresholds were for grade point average, and the level and extent of leadership and extracurricular activities needed to secure my placement?

Once you've discovered all the written rules, the next question is, *Do I understand all the written rules presented?* Each rule may have layers and involve various interpretations. Some rules may have different meanings in different countries, industries, companies, cultures, and contexts. People think language is binary, but it is not. The lens that you apply to read and interpret the rule may impact and shift how you fulfill it.

Keeping with academic examples, in the United States, HBS and Stanford Graduate School of Business (GSB) are two of the top and most popular business schools. Each of the schools publishes its admission requirements, which include completion of an undergraduate degree with a certain grade point average, passing the Graduate Management Admission Test with a minimum score, professional experience, leadership, extracurricular activities, etc. It's a common perception that the schools are similar, and the requirements are the same. Heck, even the mottos sound similar. The HBS motto is "We educate leaders who make a difference in the world,"[17] while GSB's is "Change lives. Change organizations. Change the world."[18] While on the surface the written rules for entry may appear similar, there are substantive and nuanced differences in what the admission committees look for. The contexts for the rules are different.

Many candidates spend a lot of time and money researching and understanding the fine points and layers of each requirement. They visit the campus and speak to school officials, as well as past and current students. Some may take preparatory classes or hire consultants to help with their application package. Competitive candidates check and cross-reference multiple sources of information, synthesizing all inputs to present their candidacy as prepared and knowledgeable of the rules and context of each school.

360-Degree Lens

When reading the written rules, you must analyze each rule closely. Look at it through a holistic lens. Each side may have different stakeholders and nuances that need to be addressed. Talk to others who have gone through the process. Ensure that you understand the written and verbal requirements. Take it further and look for an opportunity to do more than fulfill that written rule while also putting your own creative and innovative spin on it. Find ways to positively stand out, as my colleague from the last chapter did by submitting his analysis at 12:01 AM on May 1.

The trickier of the two types of codes to uncover is the unwritten ones, which are often the most critical to win your preferred outcome.

The Unwritten Rules

The CodeBreaker Mindset™ Equation

[(Written Rules + **Unwritten Rules**) × Pivots] $^{\text{Serendipity, Informed Intuition}}$ =

Professional Judgment and Decision

In the equation, while the unwritten rules follow the written rules, the unwritten rules are significantly more important. They may not be written down anywhere, but they are present everywhere. I challenge you to think of one area where unwritten rules don't exist. From medicine to music, engineering to sports, the world is full of hidden codes, and knowing them can be the reason why you land your dream job or inexplicably get passed over.

These undercover rules are not obvious, not plain and simple for just anyone to know and see. They do not get handed out on a silver platter. You have to search for them. This is by design. Not everyone competes at the same level. Those who want to stand out against the status quo need to prepare at a higher level.

Often, the unwritten rules are known by those born into or well exposed to privileged circumstances, and this provides a huge advantage over those who weren't. Let's call these people insiders. An insider will absorb these codes as if by osmosis. They are part of how the person thinks and behaves because they grew up immersed in the codes and environments where this was the norm. For example, insiders, in this case elite wealthy families, knew about attending private schools. In the United States, private schools began admitting lower-income students in the mid-twentieth century. More private schools started emphasizing economic diversity in their mission, beginning in the 1980s. My parents and I did not know that private schools were an option, as we were outsiders. Did you?

If being aware and exposed to unwritten rules wasn't your frame of reference growing up, it's even more important to excavate the unwritten rules rather than taking the time to explore the hidden intricacies of the written rules. Discovering them requires getting deliberate and methodical. Let's say in a strange twist of fate, someone handed you a stack of papers and said, "Here are all the unwritten rules." You might start reading and not understand them because you aren't familiar with the lingo, or don't fully comprehend the nuances of the game, context, and dynamics at play. Most, if not all, industries, companies, and contexts have a code and secret language. For example, in TV news, a common phrase is "I am crashing," which means *Don't talk to me. I am about to go on air soon, and I am rushing to get my preparation and story done.*

Let's say you're hired at a company with an open-door culture. Senior management may reiterate at company-wide meetings that they have an open-door policy that invites any employee to speak with senior executives and bring forward ideas without getting caught up in bureaucracy or hierarchy. In reality, is this true and literal? In most companies, if you were to go around your boss or leadership chain and act on that open-door policy by speaking directly with senior members, you'd likely get slapped back into place by your immediate manager, and even that same senior management. Unwritten rules can be veiled, nuanced codes, and can often lead to success or demise.

Designed to Keep You Out

Understand that the codes are designed to keep people out. There's competition for everything. Thus institutions, structures, people, and the establishment, with their scarcity mindsets in full bloom, create all sorts of rules, especially unwritten rules and filters, to keep whoever they deem less favorable out. They use assumptions that tell them the ideal candidate will look and sound a certain way, they will have gone to this school, participated in this fraternity/sorority, etc. But that homogenizes the talent pool and leaves out those who may appear different but have more talent.

Assuming who is favorable is like getting your news from social media. You focus on the sound bite but miss the substance. The more unwritten, veiled, and ambiguous the code is, the more it acts as a moving target; difficult to pin down exactly what's required to break through.

This is true in many industries and certainly for the most highly coveted jobs. It's unequivocally true in nonlinear career pivots or situations where you are an outlier. When I was breaking into TV, I was asked to submit a reel, which is a video collection of a person's reporting and anchoring. My first reel was more than five minutes long. I later learned that TV news bosses neither have time nor the attention span to watch a five-minute-plus reel. Instead, I needed to put my best reporting and anchoring shots up front and keep the reel to three minutes. The defining point here was me learning that no matter how long the reel was, I had to catch the viewer's attention instantaneously, within the first sixty seconds. This is an unwritten rule that

I learned by submitting reels and getting feedback. You can also learn this from other professionals in the industry who are generous and share tips.

Gathering the Rules

Let's look at some tactics to take inventory of the company or industry insider codes. First, ask yourself these questions:

- What are the written rules?
- What are the unwritten rules? How opaque, ambiguous, or hidden are the unwritten rules? A lack of transparency is always a red flag hiding the real motivations at play in a situation.
- How can I fully learn and understand the written or unwritten rules? Maybe it means getting some one-on-one time with a key stakeholder at the organization, in the industry, or ecosystem who can let you in on the insider know-how.
- How do I navigate around everybody else? What will make me stand out and jump ahead?

Discovering the Unwritten Rules

We'll be diving deep into how to go about information discovery in chapter 8, "Information Is Power," but let's hit a few key points here.

Know They Exist

An advantage in discovering unwritten rules is simply knowing they exist. The opportunity and competitive edge occur when you can automatically train yourself to remember they exist and then get curious about what they are. You are training and tuning your mind and analytical skills to be awake and alert.

Scour the Sources

Start uncovering the unwritten rules by searching all available sources. Competitive information exists on the edge, on the margin. To get a job in broadcast journalism, for example, you want to get in front of the decision makers who are the top executives. However, it's not enough that you have a good relationship with the head of the TV news network—the team of producers, writers, cameramen, make-up crew, and others must also like you. Find out all you can so you can make an unforgettable impression. In this context, information is gold. Information found on the margins is the concept of disintermediating information. In hedge funds and trading, financial experts make money on disintermediating information. This means capturing information in the gap, in intersections and spaces that others cannot see, are not aware of, or do not know how to read, decipher, and act on.

Quality of the Source

Talk to as many heterogenous people as you can. This is where diversity and diverse ecosystems truly come in. The more homogenous your approach is, the more consistent, standard, and status quo information you will find. This will not lead you to unearthing all the unwritten rules. A robust information discovery process will help you find the patterns and informed intuition hidden in the written and unwritten rules knitted around you, so you can then harness them for your betterment.

Try Until You Succeed

Another dimension to unwritten rules is being aware of pivots, iterations, and innovations. You'll notice pivoting is one element in The CodeBreaker Mindset™ Equation. We'll be covering the idea thoroughly in the next chapter, but let's look specifically here at how pivots impact unwritten rules.

You may have failures—things not working out the way you expected or according to plan—which require you to pivot. This is where the phrase "Try until you succeed" comes in. Part of having unwritten rules is knowing there will be times when it will be necessary for you to pivot. Instead of fearing this, reframe your mindset to see what you can learn from them. Pivots can inform and shed new and different light on the written rules and aid you in learning more about the evolving unwritten rules.

Pivots are what bring meaning to the adage that experience is the greatest teacher. What is experience? It is having the courage to try something, succeed or fail at what you tried, and then observe what you learned from the entirety of enduring it. Experiences improve and advance your understanding of any written rules, while also helping you to build a directory of unwritten codes to draw from. This is how you build pattern recognition.

Pattern Recognition

CASE STUDY

Navin Chaddha, Mayfield Fund, Managing Partner

Top-ranked venture capital investor Navin Chaddha, Managing Partner of the multi-billion-dollar firm Mayfield Fund, recognizes the importance of pattern recognition. He has backed eighteen of some of the most significant technology companies that went public, including the ride-sharing company Lyft, social commerce marketplace Poshmark, and developer tool company HashiCorp.

Drawing on his illustrious career as a multi-decade investor, appearing many times on the Forbes Midas List, including ranking in the top five multiple times, Navin enlightens on the various ways a person can learn: "You can learn from reading books, blogs, going to all the popular sites."[19] He illustrates how the lesson comes when we go to practice what we learned and burn our hands. "This is how we learn more. We learn the most from our mistakes," he says. "Then you figure out, and it's called pattern recognition, what works, what doesn't work. Hopefully, you don't make the same old mistakes. You focus on making new mistakes. Mayfield has the benefit of being an institution with fifty-plus years of pattern recognition. You learn by experience. Experience counts for something."

Hard to Codify Unwritten Rules

Mr. Chaddha elaborates on the written rules at Mayfield Fund. "Zoom in on the people," he says. "We are a people-first firm, which bets on people because they make products. Products don't make people. People build companies. Companies don't build people. So our investment lens is really figuring out the entrepreneur. Do they have it in them to create greatness? So that's the secret sauce of what we evaluate. Then we go to the problem they're trying to solve. The written rule is, are they creating the customer's painkiller or vitamin? Third, how big is this? Is it a niche that one hundred people need as a painkiller, or is it a mass-market phenomenon?"

For the unwritten rules, Mr. Chaddha admits, "We learn every day, and it's hard to codify them. We still go wrong on people. We are just trying to get better and better and better at that part of it."

The Chance Encounter—How Serendipity Impacts Unwritten Rules

Serendipity is another element of The CodeBreaker Mindset™ Equation that we'll discuss in chapter 7, "Serendipity and Informed Intuition," but let's briefly look at how serendipity impacts unwritten rules and is an unwritten rule itself. This word has different meanings to different people, cultures, and age groups, but for now, let's think of it as the nonlinear element at play in CodeBreaking. Or, put another way, a magical chance or opportune alignment of various elements.

Just imagine the tech world today had Steve Jobs and Steve Wozniak, Apple's founders, not met in a California suburb in 1971. Such a breakthrough relied entirely on their mutual friend, Bill Fernandez, who happened to live on the same block as Wozniak. Jobs was hanging out at Fernandez's house one afternoon, and they decided to take a walk around the neighborhood. They came upon Wozniak washing his car, and Bill introduced them. The rest is history. Serendipity is often at play and, thus, an unwritten code or factor.

Serendipity could mean being in the right place at the right time—having a chance to engage with a key player who can advance your career or sitting down next to someone on the subway that you end up marrying. Serendipity could show you such favor that your profile and characteristics are a better fit to fulfill the written and unwritten requirements at one point in time over another. Serendipity can create favorable circumstances to accelerate your ability to break into the insiders' circle than just about any other element in our equation. As you're discovering the unwritten rules in a selected field, be aware how serendipitous opportunities could be the gift to uncover and learn unwritten rules, or the way things really work in anything you are pursuing.

A key unwritten rule to having success at these impromptu encounters is being prepared. CodeBreaking is a way of life. It's a continuous process. Encourage yourself to always be alert. Continuously evaluate, synthesize, and do the homework. For example, before you go to a conference or event, consider who will be there. Who do you want to make sure you talk to? If a surprise person shows up, do you have your elevator pitch ready in your head for what you want to accomplish? As the popular attribution to the Roman philosopher Seneca says, "Luck is when preparation meets opportunity."

Follow or Defy the Rules

Now that we have outlined how written and unwritten rules are part of any goal you pursue, you may ask yourself, *Do I have to conform to these rules?* The answer? It depends. Certain rules in certain contexts must be followed. For example, if you want to be a doctor, you must adhere to certain prescribed education programs, exams, practical experience, and licensing. In other professions, you may have more wiggle room around both the written and unwritten tenets. In some industries, the opportunity may be ripe to not conform but defy and disrupt the paradigm to create your own new approach.

A popular example of this is social media influencers. In social media, there are certain best practices in building and executing one's brand, marketing, content creation, and paid advertising, but it's a sandbox where many of the most successful influencers came up with their own hack and system of how to go viral and attract millions of followers.

It's not about following or conforming per se. The value is in being informed to formulate your own ingredients and sequence of steps that will lead you to a path of victory and achievement.

Don't Be Played—Know the Written and Unwritten Rules

Whether it's in the "little" or "big" leagues, knowing the written and unwritten codes in any situation will help you avoid getting played. Similarly, the dynamics in the animal kingdom are characterized by a predator-prey relationship. So too it goes in the human jungle, as we'll see in the following real-life Hollywood saga.

CASE STUDY

Kazembe Ajamu, 5Tre The Blade, Founder and CEO; Father of Zendaya

Kazembe Ajamu, educator, media executive, and founder/CEO of 5Tre The Blade, is beyond battle-tested in the global entertainment industry. The father of global prodigious superstar Zendaya, he orchestrated roughly the first twenty years of her journey and career. This included teaching her critical life skills, and developing, supporting, and managing her talent from childhood to adulthood in areas such as modeling, music, television, film, as well as global strategic brand and business partnerships. While it may appear that Zendaya effortlessly rose to critical and commercial stardom with a social media following in the hundreds of millions, she and her family, being new to Hollywood, had to learn to maneuver that jungle.

Zendaya

The written and unwritten rules morphed as Kazembe guided his daughter through the convoluted maze of ever-increasing stardom, from modeling shoots for brands like Macy's to commercial sets such as a Sears ad featuring Selena Gomez where Zendaya was a backup dancer, to gaining global recognition through multiple Disney Channel TV shows and films, especially *Shake It Up*, and eventually soaring to global blockbuster films like Marvel Studios' *Spider-Man: Homecoming*.

On achieving celebrity, fame, and wealth, Kazembe highlights, "People think you're rich just because you're on television. They think you're making a lot of money. Especially if you land a TV series. So do you until you see the check. Once you see the check, you're like, f***, this is the same amount of money we're making as teachers.

"The depth of the screwing is beyond your imagination. They make you famous, and they want you to show up. Zendaya had to show up to all of these events, do red carpets, and conduct interviews. Well, I asked a question: 'What is she going to wear? Who's paying for what she's wearing? Who pays for all of this?' So when they start creating a celebrity, they are supposed to pay for some of it, but they only pay for what's important to them. There's no real budget for you to self-promote. If they want you to go to something, they don't want to pay for it. They just want you to show up and take pictures and do interviews. That cost came out of our pockets."

Disney Rules

"Working with Disney was financially overwhelming at times," he explains. "We are talking about the rules of the game. Disney offers you a contract that's non-negotiable. There is no negotiating with Disney. You take it or leave it. If you don't like it, they have a thousand kids that would come on Disney Channel and work for free and gladly take your place.

"Zendaya had booked the show, and Disney wanted her. I could not 'negotiate' the contract with Disney, as agents are needed to do that. The agent got 10 percent for doing nothing, as he didn't negotiate anything whatsoever. We didn't know that at the time. I'm sure the agents, managers, and lawyers knew the dynamics, but I didn't know.

"Looking at the money side, let's say 10 percent goes to the agent, 10 percent goes to the manager, 5 percent goes to the attorney, another 5 percent goes to the publicist, 15 percent goes to the tax authorities. 45 percent of her money is gone before she sees a dime. Also, 15 percent goes to the Coogan account."[20]

Celebrity Wealth

Kazembe realized that while being a Disney actor had helped Zendaya achieve celebrity, its strict contract terms did not make things financially sustainable.

Zendaya was around fourteen years old when Disney's *Shake It Up* exploded. "Her trajectory was growing at warp speed. It was a good-paying gig. As that celebrity grew, the paychecks didn't get any bigger because the contract was fixed. Disney owns you, owns your name and likeness. You can't do anything without Disney's permission. Disney isn't going to permit you to do anything other than promote and do Disney."

The media and entertainment giant heavily promoted *Shake It Up* globally, creating dolls of Zendaya and her co-star Bella Thorne. Kazembe says,

"Disney made millions of dollars from selling merchandise globally with these two girls. For roughly every $20 sold, the two girls earned half a cent each."

As the show skyrocketed in popularity and Zendaya was extensively involved in promotions, Kazembe "started asking questions and asking for audits. 'Shouldn't we be getting paid for this?' he asked. She got one check for $50,000, and they refused to let our attorneys audit the books."

Street Smarts

"Celebrity may not make you rich," Kazembe says. "Half the people that you see, even today, on television, if you're not the star or lead, and you're somebody else, they're probably living in some little apartment somewhere, barely scraping by.

"I had to figure out how to parlay the celebrity into a check to keep us here in Hollywood and living. In the beginning, we did a lot of appearances and a lot of autograph signings. We did them all over the country. I had the hustle to create things outside of the Disney contractual constraints where Zendaya could be. She would come and sign hundreds, sometimes a thousand autographs, and appear at shows, fairs, carnivals, schools. We may have done something for $500, then $1,000, $2,000. Then as her celebrity grew, the price went up to $5,000, $10,000, $20,000, $100,000. Hell, now, it probably cost a couple million dollars to get her."

Everyone is a prey to learning and maneuvering written and unwritten rules, from those who operate in quiet life paradigms to the glamorous worlds of the rich and famous.

Now, you're well on your way to developing the mindset and skills to think like a CodeBreaker. In the next chapter, we'll take a more in-depth look at pivots and the role they play in your quest for success.

The CodeBreaker Mindset™ Takeaways

- Be aware of and embrace the fact that every goal involves some sort of game that has written and unwritten rules that inform how to play and advance. Make sure that you know what the game is, you are in it, and you equip yourself to compete.
- A key universal written and unwritten rule is to always be alert and prepared.
- Learn the written and unwritten rules and develop the pattern recognition, so you won't be played.

Chapter 5

Pivots Part I: When the Siege Comes

> If you even dream of beating me, you'd better wake up and apologize.[21]
>
> —Muhammad Ali, boxing legend, three-time World Heavyweight Champion

The CodeBreaker Mindset™ Equation

[(Written Rules + Unwritten Rules) × **Pivots**]$^{\text{Serendipity, Informed Intuition}}$ =

Professional Judgment and Decision

How often has your career or life unfolded in a straight path versus twists and turns in the journey? These maneuvers are called pivots. There are two types of pivots: voluntary and involuntary. Involuntary pivots are fondly known as hijacks. Hijacks interrupt. They push us off course and force us to change our expectations or desired trajectory. When we're hijacked, we have to pivot, or we die.

Pivots are such a critical component to The CodeBreaker Mindset™ Equation that I've broken the discussion into two chapters. In this chapter, we'll look closely at external hijacks and how we can be prepared when the unexpected interrupts our linear flow. I'll show you how to read the signals, which are indicators of potential pivots that may occur, so you aren't caught off guard when it comes time to pivot. In the next chapter, we'll spend time addressing how to build your pivot muscle and the pattern recognition to spot possible pivots, ways to regain your power when it's been taken from you, and how to emotionally care for yourself in the aftermath of a hijack.

Unfair and surprise situations require you to pivot. You know this; you've been pivoting your whole life, whether you knew it or not. Pivots change our linear path and can force a nonlinear direction. Understanding pivots is essential to being the master of your destiny. Don't let pivots sabotage, paralyze, or victimize you. Get ahead of the pivots and own them. This chapter will teach you how.

Hijacks come in a variety of forms, but at the core, a hijacker steals from, robs, or coerces a person or situation. In the professional world, a hijacker will behave in a way that is inappropriate, unwarranted, or unmerited, which can leave you feeling unsettled or resentful.

A hijack may not be a person but a situation. You may not get the promotion you worked for and objectively earned. Perhaps you are inappropriately passed over for a prime position or don't receive the merit-based raise that you earned. Or the company steals your idea and doesn't give you credit.

Self-Sabotage

We can also hijack ourselves. It's called self-sabotage when we consciously or subconsciously do things that disturb or hinder our ability to achieve our goals. For instance, when you have a big meeting or test, but you stay out late the night before, don't get sufficient rest, or don't prepare thoroughly, that's self-sabotage.

Have you ever *not* wanted to attend an event, so you don't give yourself sufficient travel time and end up arriving late? You could have easily avoided it but didn't. That's hijacking yourself. We are all guilty of self-sabotage to varying degrees. These events are controllable and avoidable, and you can work to remedy them.

For this chapter, we will be focusing not on self-sabotage, but on when the hijacks come externally. In this chapter, we also won't be focusing on positive pivots, such as when a boss sponsors, mentors, promotes, and gives you an opportunity. He or she may actively help you architect your career and progression. Hallelujah for those scenarios, but I don't know about you—most people I know rarely find such magical figures in their lives.

Hijacks: The Involuntary Pivot

The hard truth is, you're going to get hijacked over and over during your life. It's unavoidable. The upside is that you'll be in good company because everyone deals with this. A hijacking may be perpetrated by one person or several. The other person(s) may feel justified in their actions. If you take the time to study them, you may realize it is within the scope of their nature and behavior to hijack people.

Wall Street Hijacking

For some, they may not like or want to be the perpetrator of the hijacking, but they may feel they have no other choice. A painful example of this for me was many years ago when I worked in a bank. The Managing Director (MD) in the group (let's call her Sarah) told me my performance was stellar and asked about my career aspirations in front of my immediate manager (let's call her Mary).

I was less experienced in the ways of the corporate world and felt excited that I was being asked this by the leader of our group, so I naively told both of them my goals. My immediate manager shot back, "You don't get to do that until I do."

I smiled and said, "Okay, sure." I did not think anything of it and figured my merit would speak for itself. I did not know that "little" conversation would be a turning point, a slow death, for me.

A few months later, when I received my performance evaluation, it said I was a low performer and listed a number of false statements. I was horrified. Another colleague was asked to support the false assertions in my review. That colleague felt she had no choice but to go along with what my manager and the MD were putting in the review because the MD was seen as a powerful person. While the MD and my boss hijacked me, that employee contributed to the hijacking. It was painful. I was crushed. I worked in an organization and group where such false assertions could be made by managers who got away with it. Friends, this is very common anywhere in the world.

I knew I had to move out of the group. I was already internally networked in the organization and worked quickly to move away from these disingenuous and dangerous folks. The treachery didn't end there—giving me such a bad review in writing meant they were setting me up to be let go.

I was able to figure this out through analyzing all that was going on, but especially through talking to three other senior leaders in the company, outside of my group, who imparted insights on what Sarah and Mary were trying to do. Yes, we want to keep our dramas private, but we can't know everything. I was not able to fully "read the tea leaves," as they say, or understand the severity and order of magnitude of what was happening. Having senior colleagues who've proven themselves trustworthy and provide genuine mentorship can offer wise and needed counsel.

I trusted these three senior leaders and told them candidly what had happened. They each told me in various ways that I needed to exit my group. I started networking to move myself.

I was able to pivot and go work for another leader in the same company (let's call him Mark). Per protocol, I told my existing manager, Mary, that I'd gotten a new job and would be making an internal transfer. This was fully permitted per company rules. Since Sarah and Mary did not like me, for whatever reason, and Mary felt threatened, they should have been thrilled that I was leaving on my own.

They were not. They tried to destroy me. Destroy is a strong word, right? It fits. Sarah proactively called Mark and spoke ill of me, hoping to dissuade him from hiring me. Mark did not listen to her and proceeded with my transfer.

At my one-year anniversary of working for Mark, he gave me an outstanding ranking in every category on my performance review. He said in my review that I was instrumental to his and the group's success. He also gave me the largest pay increase I'd ever had in that company (as I had been underpaid).

Mark was willing to go against a fellow department head and give me a shot because he understood what was going on. He had been in the organization a long time and was more aware than I was of Sarah being a hazardous operative. Mark had also done internal background checks on me prior to offering me the job and had received positive feedback from other Managing Directors. He gave me the benefit of the doubt, took a risk, and it paid off . . . for him and me. Mark and I are still in touch to this day, and every year on his birthday, I tell him he is the best boss I've ever had.

How often in your life have you had someone, personally or professionally, stand up for you? Consider it a blessing and a gift when it happens because it's rare.

In varying degrees, we have all been in this type of scenario, whether personally or professionally. It can break your spirit. Thank you to all the Marks out there who operate more on merit and integrity rather than mediocrity and politics.

This situation was both a voluntary and an involuntary pivot, simultaneously. The involuntary part of this pivot was Sarah and Mary hijacking me. However, before they could eject me from the company, the ultimate involuntary pivot, I moved myself. I found a promising opportunity with Mark and voluntarily pivoted myself to him, before I was pushed out by Sarah and Mary.

This is the value in being aware and building the pivot muscle, which we'll discuss in the next chapter. If you can read and get ahead of the signals in a dangerous situation and relocate yourself to safety on your terms, then you have taken back your power. You've taken the power away from the hijacker and shifted yourself before they could continue to harm you.

Pivots in Business Are Standard

Companies, CEOs, senior executives, and team members face continuous pivots in business. This is the norm. The pivots are motivated by an unlimited population of factors such as changes in leaders and teams, the economy, regulation and policy, competitors, customers, availability of inputs and resources, business model, taxation, labor, etc. The more you are prepared for changes in any of these factors, through conducting different permutations and combinations of risk and scenario planning, the more agile, versatile, and quicker you will be to respond to the storms in the oceans of business.

Amazon

Let's look at Amazon, one of the world's highest valued companies, as an example. When Amazon first burst onto the scene in 1995, it sold books online, giving itself the moniker of "Earth's Biggest Bookstore." At first, Amazon focused on competing with brick-and-mortar retailers like Barnes & Noble and Waldenbooks. In 1997, when Amazon went public, no one could predict it would one day dominate e-commerce and cloud computing.

Amazon launched its marketplace in 2000, which let third parties list items online. This offered consumers greater selection and gave Amazon a dramatic jump in revenue. The third-party marketplace, combined with Amazon directly selling more than just books, made Amazon the go-to online retailer. In 2006, Amazon expanded, adding cloud computing services, becoming a leader in the industry. Not giving up on books, Amazon released the e-reader, Kindle, that same year. Over the next decade, Amazon continued to diversify, acquiring companies like Audible and Whole Foods, and launching physical stores. It entered the streaming war with Amazon Instant Video, which has evolved into Prime Video, to compete against Netflix.[22]

Innovation, reinvention, evolution, and diversification are all part of the normal population of changes and pivots that for-profit and nonprofit enterprises make. Some are sparked by creativity, accident, or necessity. Irrespective of the reason, the five agents of chaos only make the ability of any organization to pivot itself before being disrupted by others more critical.

CASE STUDY

Ken Ohashi, Brooks Brothers, CEO

Pandemic Pivot

Ken Ohashi became the CEO of the iconic American high-end fashion retailer Brooks Brothers in the fall of 2020 during the global COVID-19 pandemic. The company, which was founded in 1818 and at one time was a multi-billion-dollar brand, had filed for bankruptcy in the summer of 2020. Multi-billion-dollar brand management company Authentic Brands Group (which owns Nautica, Nine West, Vince Camuto, Forever 21, as well as the intellectual property for David Beckham, Muhammad Ali, Elvis, and Marilyn Monroe), along with Simon Property Group, bought Brooks Brothers in the summer of 2020.

After a distinguished career as a consumer and retail leader at firms such as Aeropostale and Authentic Brands Group, Ken had a vision for Brooks Brothers. After discussing his plans with Authentic Brands Group Chairman and CEO Jamie Salter, Ken was tapped to be CEO. He led the heavy turnaround work, lifting the company back to profitability in four years.

Monday to Sunday Clothing

On pivoting Brooks Brothers, Ken spoke about the climate of clothing in the middle of the pandemic, when no one was buying suits or dress shirts, saying, "The majority of the business was dress shirts and suits, but everybody was moving into casual wear and sweatpants. Lululemon was hot. The major pivot we made was swinging the business from being 18 percent casual when I got here—chinos and casual Friday sort of apparel—to hiring Michael Bastian [Creative Director] as part of that journey to establish casual elements for Brooks Brothers. We now offer Monday through Sunday clothing. Forty-five percent of our business is what I consider casual. That was a big pivot. Because it's not just about design. It's whether we can have the factories produce it. Do we understand the fabrics? Then we have to look at if the store teams know how to sell it. We had to make that pivot all the way down the entire organization."

I talked to Ken about the creative aspect and how spotting trends before others do is another form of pivoting, as is deciding new directions for your enterprise. Ken emphasizes, "Every single piece of our business has a creative component. In the product design piece, Michael balances looking forward while also looking back. The beauty of Brooks Brothers is that we have two hundred years of history. Part of the journey was looking back to move forward and understanding what worked well historically. This year, we relaunched our collegiate, back-to-campus campaign. Back in the 1960s, '70s, and '80s, Brooks Brothers was a destination for Ivy League students going back to campus. We're bringing those elements back. We're looking in unconventional places for inspiration, and that has unlocked a huge vault of ideas."

Ken Ohashi orchestrated big and small pivots at Brooks Brothers out of necessity, creativity, and innovation, resulting in reinventing the brand to relevance and leaping from bankruptcy to profitability.

Hijacks Happen. What Happens Next Is on You.

Hijacks are a normal part of our personal and professional lives. You're going to get hijacked, probably many times. This is partly due to human nature and the notion of survival of the fittest. It's also because with chaos being the new norm, competition is heightened, and the written and unwritten rules for success have been obliterated. It's crucial to be educated to spot hijacks early and neutralize them.

Be Aware

Hone the fine art of *awareness*. You don't want to be caught off guard or surprised when something in your life or career goes awry. When a hijack happens out of the blue, it can disrupt you *badly*. It's difficult enough to figure out how to change course once your preferred trajectory gets interrupted, but it's even harder to do so when you never saw it coming!

Your goal is to master the art of being both engaged in your work and aware of what people and your environment are showing you. Be all in and at the same time, keep an eye on the terrain and horizon. People are constantly signaling their intentions through their words, actions, body language, and explicit or subtle behaviors (or the absence thereof). Organizations are also sending signs and information through their stakeholders, processes, systems, culture, and in the way they operate and conduct business. If you pay attention, you will start to pick up on the indicators.

Ask yourself continuously, *Do the actions of stakeholders match their words?* Observe and track the results over a period of time. Compare your notes with those you trust. You are looking to uncover if the words and actions are consistent, and thus the substance matches the form. Inconsistencies, especially those that are frequent, pervasive, or material, can be signs that hijacks are in flight.

CodeBreakers Handle Hijacks Differently

Who enjoys being hijacked? No one. It can feel cruel, hurtful, disappointing, and unfair. It may cause your quality of life to plummet and fill you with self-doubt or despair. When you get hijacked, it is easy to ask, *Why me?* Rather than sinking into a trench of self-pity, sadness, or anger, I'll show you how to handle the hijack like a CodeBreaker and avoid being demolished.

CodeBreakers pivot to something better. If pivoting to something better is not possible, they pivot to something that keeps them moving forward—whatever it takes to not stay stuck and spinning their wheels.

Learn to Read the Signals

Signals, patterns of signals, and data analysis are critical and ultimately separate those who survive, thrive, and win from those who don't. A big part of being a CodeBreaker is reading the explicit and subtle indicators because they help you understand the macro-to-micro picture. These signals can tell you whether you are in or on the out, whether you are on the rise, the decline, or irrelevant.

Earlier in my life and career, I was naïve to think that a person always meant what they said—that their thoughts, words, and actions were always in alignment. Many of us have learned the hard way that what people say to our faces often does not align with their true intentions and actions.

Let's say your boss claims to be thrilled with your work in a performance review but lays you off one month later. That can sting and catch you off guard. But what if you had known ahead of time that even though your boss liked you well enough, they were also sponsoring and advocating for two other employees on your team? Your eventual layoff might have been less of a shock, and you might have had the foresight to put out a few feelers in the meantime, or to at least start thinking about your next move.

Observing the explicit and subtle behaviors of stakeholders and key individuals, understanding how the winds and currents in your environment are shifting, and connecting all these data dots can lift you steps ahead of assault. They can help you maneuver the intersections of siege. In the next chapter, using a work and career context, we'll learn about some of the key categories of signals, how to interpret them, and what they could mean, so you aren't caught in a field of land mines.

The CodeBreaker Mindset™ Takeaways

- Pivots, both voluntary and involuntary, are a part of everyday life and have been present in your entire personal and professional journey.
- Observe the data and pattern recognition from people, situations, and experiences that signal the need to pivot to get ahead of intersections of siege or how to maneuver if you are hijacked.
- Informed intuition can sharpen your ability to sense the arrival of voluntary and involuntary pivots because they are a source of knowledge from accumulated pattern recognition, which is housed in your intuition (more on this in chapter 7, "Serendipity and Informed Intuition").

Chapter 6

Pivots Part II: Maneuver the Intersections of Siege

> When someone shows you who they are, believe them the first time.[23]
>
> —Maya Angelou, award-winning poet and three-time Grammy Award recipient

The CodeBreaker Mindset™ Equation

[(Written Rules + Unwritten Rules) × **Pivots**] $^{\text{Serendipity, Informed Intuition}}$ =

Professional Judgment and Decision

In the last chapter, we discussed that pivots are standard in business and life, and increasing in frequency and severity given the agents of chaos. Whether internal or external, voluntary or involuntary, you don't have to be an unsuspecting victim. The opportunity available is to anticipate a hijack by spotting and decoding the signals and fortifying yourself to get ahead of or take the pivots head on. Don't let the pivots seize and siege you.

Your ability to pivot improves with practice. Like a muscle, it grows stronger and more flexible when exercised regularly. Using the work environment as our stage, in this chapter, we'll learn to examine the messaging and behavior of company leadership, coworkers, and colleagues to detect what may be covert red flags foretelling an imminent hijack. Will you see the signs and weather the attack, or are you distracted and leaving yourself vulnerable to the coming storm?

KYE: Know Your Environment

In a career, your environment consists of the industry, company, and various stakeholders such as competitors, clients, vendors, industry organizations, professional bodies, etc. It's an ecosystem.

Know Your Ecosystem and Industry Thoroughly

Many people do not have a thorough understanding of what's going on in their industry. Ignorance may be bliss, but it won't help you when a major disruption or blow makes you vulnerable or sidelines you.

Here are some starting points for gaining a comprehensive knowledge of your career ecosystem:

- Learn all you can about the macro- and microeconomic factors impacting your industry.
- Study what's going on inside your organization and with competitors.
- Read what external stakeholders are communicating about your industry and company, whether that's from the media, press, or social media.

- For publicly traded companies, read your company's annual report and external filings, as well as the annual reports of competitors and other key stakeholders in your industry. If your company is privately owned, or public information is not available, find information on other similar stakeholders in the ecosystem so you can develop relevant and contextual knowledge.
- Familiarize yourself with the financial statements, if they are available.
- Listen to the earnings call and read the transcript, where available, especially for publicly traded companies.
- Absorb the same for competitors and other key stakeholders in your industry.
- Consume everything on your company's internal and external website and social media channels.
- Attend the town halls and listen closely to what's being said and what's not being said.
- Be aware of the talk around the office. Look for data to substantiate what you are hearing informally from colleagues. Rumors may or may not be true. All this intel will help identify signals that could indicate if there are elevated risks and issues in your industry and company.

Know Your Company

Knowing your industry gives you power. The next step is to be a student of your company. What follows are a few ideas to help you sleuth out more intel:

- Stay on top of company news, organizational changes, performance results, key client wins and losses and their implications for revenue and pressure on expenses, etc.

- Be able to identify who the senior management and key players in the organization are, by face and name. I meet many individuals who do not know the names of the CEO and C-Suite executives at their firm, nor what they look like. If you don't know the basics, you are not in the game.
- Understand the macro- and microeconomic impacts on your company, such as interest rates, inflation, foreign exchange rates, as well as the cost and availability of raw materials, supply chain, talent, any inputs to your business, etc.
- Is your company facing any scandals, setbacks, reputational risks, litigation, regulatory issues, and/or fines? How will it pay for any losses? What are the repercussions and outcomes of any of these risks and issues?
- Who will be affected if there are job cuts?
- Do you work in a cost center or revenue center? Often, when there are issues, those who work in cost centers are impacted first, as there is a perception that those jobs are a lower priority than revenue-generating jobs.

Know That Layoffs Are the Norm

Layoffs are common, even in companies that are doing well. This isn't surprising given the chaos and disruption era we're all battling through. AI is replacing, reclassifying, or changing jobs across several industries. Most organizations are looking to cut costs. Regardless of the reasons, the days of working forty years for the same company and retiring with a gold watch are over. (You already knew that, of course, but it's really hitting home now.) Chances are, you're going to be laid off at some point, if you haven't been already.

Think about it for a moment. It's the law of gravity. What goes up will come down. When you join a company, even if you are a high performer and have sponsorship, your trajectory will rise, but eventually it will plateau. You won't know how long the rise or the plateau will last. Even if you plateau, you may have other upward rises. Take and enjoy all the rises you can get, as well as the plateaus. They won't last forever, even if you have the best sponsor or work for the CEO of the organization.

Of course, if you're lucky and super connected, your journey may go on indefinitely. However, most people—especially those without connections or sponsorship—will eventually be let go, either through a structured or one-off layoff process, or via a political hijacking. If you're prepared for this eventuality, you'll be less surprised and better able to plan and carry out your next move.

Synthesize the Signals

Tie together all the environmental signals that we have discussed and reflect on how they jive with all that you have observed and tabulated around you. How are the economy, industry, company, and competitors performing? Are there macro- or micro-headwinds impacting any stakeholder in the value chain? Did the company give out healthy bonuses this year? Did you benefit from a nice pay bump? Were you rewarded for bringing in that important new client? Are you receiving positive feedback from your bosses? Are you and others in your peer group being promoted?

Signals like these may indicate that your company is on a growth trajectory and riding the momentum. A feeling of general optimism about the future infuses the air. This might be a good time to lean in harder, apply for that new position, ask for that raise, and move on up!

On the other hand, if your organization is struggling, the context and day-to-day culture may seem off. Here are some examples of what this can look like:

- The general demeanor of your leadership chain, manager, or colleagues may come across as unsettled, unstable, and may range from less than positive to even grim.
- There may be layoffs, whether one-offs, in small numbers, or in a more structured way.
- Talent may be leaving on their own.
- You may witness other people being hijacked.
- A hiring freeze may be in place.
- Negative sentiments may be coming in from external constituents such as clients, vendors, strategic partners, or competitors.
- The company or your business unit may put budget cutbacks in place, and pre-approval is required for all expenses, such as travel and entertainment. Budgets for attending conferences or client-related expenses are cut, put on hold, or receive extra scrutiny.

These are some clues that your job and future growth prospects at that company may be at risk. Your next step should be to validate these data points. Determine if other data points corroborate or substantiate your assessment. Look at everything together and compare, not in silos, to determine if it all adds up. Then, make the judgment call based on the situation. From there, determine what this means for you. Is your job and growth at risk? How do you want to operate going forward? Do you want to hold tight and see how it plays out? If your job is cut, perhaps you'll get severance. Do you want to formulate your exit strategy and find new opportunities? Do you want to do both? In that case, you can start while waiting to see how things play out. Your thoughts and actions don't have to be binary or discrete, but can be concurrent. This is part of risk mitigation and having a diversified plan of action.

A common miscalculation is thinking that because we do an excellent job, or because the company is doing well, we don't need to worry. Not that

I want any one of us to worry, but it pays to be aware and on guard. Don't allow yourself to be complacent and not actively observe your environment at all times. The winds can change at any time with no notice or warning. Building a muscle of active awareness helps you not be caught off guard or paralyzed if something untoward happens.

Another flawed assumption is believing that because your management chain or peers give you positive feedback, you are safe. There is no "safe." What keeps people in their jobs is not fully dependent on merit or being a high performer. Other dimensions influence retention. The challenge is to identify and understand the factors and their corresponding signals, then synthesize and evaluate that body of information so you can make a judgment call on the level of probability of being hijacked and how it will manifest.

Awareness enables you to make your own calculations, voluntarily pivot yourself out on your own terms, and remain in control.

KYP: Know Your People

When it comes to hijacking, I can't emphasize enough the importance of the following statement: We are not hijacked by *objects*, we are hijacked by people. They may show up as the elephant in the room . . . or crouch low and be as silent as a tiger . . . or anything in between.

Given that chaos is the new norm—which has resulted in increased competition in most, if not all, facets of life—it breeds a scarcity mindset in people everywhere (yourself included). A scarcity mindset can also foster a lack of trust, safety, and security. We mentioned the erosion of values and trust among people earlier when listing the agents of chaos in chapter 1.

This combination of circumstances may cause a person to focus on self-preservation or preserving those in their close inner circles and tribes. As a result, people's codes of conduct have more variability, which impacts how they show up, how helpful they are, whether they operate with integrity, and their degree of professionalism.

Here are some scenarios that describe how people might hijack you.

Be on the Lookout for Favoritism of All Kinds

Even the most well-meaning leader sometimes struggles to treat their team members with independence, objectivity, and impartiality. They are human too. Unfortunately, when you notice your leader bestowing favoritism on certain employees, it might mean you don't always receive the merit-based outcomes you have earned. When this occurs (and it likely will happen at some point in your career), remember that some outcomes have nothing to do with you or your performance.

Try not to take it personally. Favoritism exists in most workplaces, as well as in schools, volunteerism, communities, and in most, if not all, life contexts. Sometimes, decision makers simply choose their favorites over you, even if you have the best education or the perfect credentials. Other factors, like nepotism or having friends in high places, can also impact a leader's decision to promote or champion one employee over another. There may be nothing you can do to improve your place in the pecking order, but it's useful to be aware of these forces and headwinds, know where you stand, and have plans on how to maneuver accordingly.

Be Aware That Not All Bosses Give It to You Straight

Don't be surprised if you get mixed signals from your managers throughout your career. You might have a boss who smiles in your face and then recommends you for the next round of layoffs. This isn't fair, but it happens all the time.

You are likely to have bosses who are not up front with you about where you stand. In some cases, their hands are tied, and they can't be transparent with you because someone above them is the decision maker. In others, a leader might choose not to advocate for you because they don't have the bandwidth to do so, along with everything else that they're juggling. That manager may also lack the bandwidth because perhaps their job is at risk, because they are not politically in favor, or because they may be advocating for other employees who are higher in the pecking order. Finally, some employers just don't want to be the bad person, so they let you believe you're golden until the day you get your termination slip.

Consider these questions:

- Is the culture of your industry and company one of transparency?
- Do management and leaders demonstrate transparency around, for example, base salary and bonus compensation structures? Promotion processes? Requirements to be awarded more responsibilities and critical assignments?
- Do you know the criteria to qualify for professional education, training programs, international assignments, etc.?

If the culture of your industry, company, management, leaders, and teams is not transparent, then don't be surprised if your boss isn't transparent with you, either.

We've all encountered passive-aggressive behavior. Your job is to identify if that is a consistent trait in your work environment, especially with your managers. If it is, read into the passive-aggressiveness to determine what the other person is really trying to convey.

I'm not telling you not to trust your boss. But have a realistic, 360-degree view of all the factors and influences they may be dealing with, as well as their personality and style of communication. They, like you, are juggling office politics and working in a hierarchy with many different layers and levels of power and influence. They're playing the game too.

Remember, It's All Relative

No matter how good you are at your job, you won't always be the best or most liked person on every team. Think of your career in terms of your relative power, influence, and likability. Even if you are well-liked and successful, there will always be people who are more so. Your talent is relative to the other people in your orbit and whatever attributes may be prioritized at that time for whatever reason. Instead of competing with them, compete with yourself, and when you get signals that you may not be the top person, try very hard not to take it personally. It's not always personal.

Do the Signals Add Up? Does the Substance Match the Form?

Once you identify, monitor, and take in the signals, the next step involves asking yourself how it all adds up. What does your intuition or gut say? All these factors are valuable data points. Take them in. Triangulate them. Octagonulate them. (For more on octagonulate, see chapter 8, "Information Is Power.")

Figure out what may be missing. The key question you should always ask yourself is, *Does the substance match the form?* In other words, does your synthesis and analysis from the signals you have observed through your five senses align with your actual experience? Your actual experience equates to the way you are substantively and continuously treated.

Here is a guide to determine whether the substance matches the form:

- Your manager says one thing or treats you a certain way that is not consistent with your compensation, promotion, or upward mobility.
- Your manager's boss has a different view and assessment of you than your own manager.
- You are given a role but do not have the appropriate authority, empowerment, budget, team, support, or sponsorship to match.
- Your reporting line is ambiguous. When push comes to shove, who will claim you as their employee and stand up for you?

- Your employment agreements, which detail your base salary, variable compensation, and equity/stock, are not transparent, clear, or complete.
- You are left out of critical meetings, conferences, and information loops.
- Elements of your role and responsibilities are taken away from you with no substantive or merit-driven explanation.
- You are not receiving private or public credit for your work and accomplishments. Credit is being inappropriately given to others.
- Your manager or management chain has hijacked or mistreated others.

Don't think you are immune to this treatment. When a person, collective, or company shows you who they are, believe them. If they can treat someone else poorly, they can and *will* do it to you!

These are just a few examples of substance not matching form. In the short term, discovering this kind of disconnect allows you to voice your concern to your manager so it can be resolved. It could be due to an innocent oversight, or a gap due to timing or other moving factors in your organization. This can occur naturally in day-to-day business and need not cause alarm. However, over time, if there are a number of unresolved "substance versus form" gaps, these are messages for you to remain alert to your environment. You will detect a pattern, one for you to analyze and then act on. When a clear understanding of where you stand finally emerges, you'll be ready to take the appropriate action. In some cases, that might mean interviewing at other places and eventually leaving, or staying and waiting for a severance package.

Signals are invaluable. Consider it intel when observing how people and the surroundings show up. They are providing information about how others think of you and treat you—or how they will one day.

Whatever you do, don't ignore the signals. Information is power because it helps you plan how you want to navigate in that environment or work on your diversification and exit strategy.

Building the Pivot Muscle

If you think about it, we pivot all the time, every day. For example, when one potential client rejects your sales offer, what do you do? You come up with another sales pitch. Or you pivot to the next prospect. If you fail to prove your point in a debate with a colleague, you learn from the gaps, do a little more preparation, and then pick up the debate the next time.

Pivots are a part of a healthy life. If we did not regroup and try something new when faced with everyday obstacles, our opportunities and experiences would drastically shrink. Growth is all about trying new things and taking intentional steps in the direction we want to go.

Since you've already been pivoting your entire life, it shouldn't be too much of a leap to embrace larger, more impactful pivots—the kinds that drastically reshape your life for the better. Perhaps it's calling a headhunter once you recognize that you might need to leave your organization. Or going on a handful of informational interviews when considering a career shift. Or leaving your firm to work for a competitor when you have hit a ceiling in your current position.

Pivots are nothing to be afraid of. Sure, they can feel uncomfortable, especially if you're not accustomed to taking bold, decisive action, but they aren't inherently as dangerous as many people believe them to be.

Here's some advice for building the pivot muscle.

Building the Pivot Muscle: Pivot Plan. Pivot Often.

Extreme high velocity change is impacting all organizations, contexts, and people. What this means for the people in those firms (i.e., you and your colleagues) is more frequent hijackings and more occurrences of outcomes not matching expectations. This will result in more pivots for you. This isn't your mother's or father's work environment. It's a whole new world of disruption, and all CodeBreakers should embrace the pivot rather than run from it.

The earlier in life we learn and accept this, the earlier we start to build the pivot muscle. Imagine all the chaos you would have avoided if you had learned this in high school. What about learning it in elementary school? It's possible to teach our children that pivoting is part of life and not something to run from, but to get good at.

Pivoting Is Problem-Solving

Pivoting is problem-solving. Plan A didn't work, so you develop and pursue plan B. If someone tries to block you, find someone else to help or go another route. If you tried to build a relationship with a key person you thought would help you achieve your goals, but that person turns out to be unhelpful, find someone else. It's an obstacle for you to move around, or an opportunity to find another path. Don't let anything or anyone make you feel like it's the end.

There is no one golden person or path to help you achieve your objectives. Society can be heartless and leave you feeling deficient if things don't turn out your way or if you deviate from your set plan. It's mentally and emotionally easier for people to point the finger at you rather than acknowledge the nature and scope of hijackings and admit the extent to which they occur. It's mentally and emotionally convenient, and politically correct, to pretend that hijackings don't occur, and that what happened to you was merit-driven or justified. I flag this because the environment and people around you may not be encouraging you to build that pivot muscle.

Further, don't be paralyzed by the hijacking. This may be easier said than done. We've all been there and know how hard it can be when you get thrown off course. But the more you work on your pivot muscle, which starts with your mindset, the better you will get over time. Eventually, when a hijacking occurs, you won't be paralyzed. You may need to take some time to process your emotions and disappointment and recover, but you won't be destroyed. You will already have backup plans in place and the ability to move into problem-solving mode.

Risk Mitigation and Diversification

Pivoting is diversification and risk mitigation. Have allies you can turn to who can help you plot those backup plans. The more diverse your ecosystem of relationships, knowledge, and resources, the more options, ideas, and creativity you can arm yourself with to architect future steps.

Study Other People's Pivots

When we look at successful people, we often assume they had linear paths to get to where they are today. The reality is that everyone has zigzagged through life. Study and analyze others' journeys—especially those of people who inspire you. They could be friends, family members, acquaintances, CEOs, celebrities, athletes, or influencers. Inevitably, their careers and lives are comprised of a series of thoughtfully executed and impromptu pivots. There's rich data and information in their journeys. Combing through their stories, you will gain pattern recognition on how, when, and why they pivoted, and that can inform and evolve your CodeBreaker Mindset™ Equation.

This is also a source of self-empowerment, because it shows you that the paths of those you admire were not linear. They endured difficulty, recovered, and progressed to greatness. So can you.

CASE STUDY

Reshma Saujani, Girls Who Code and Moms First, Founder

Reshma Saujani, the founder of Girls Who Code and Moms First, is a leader who has owned voluntary and involuntary pivots many times. In 2009, she was the first South Asian woman to ever run for United States Congress. Reshma shares, "It was the most powerful, impactful ten months of my life. I lost that race spectacularly, but as part of that experience, I witnessed the technology divide in computer science and coding. It was 2010; that was when tech was starting to be hot like Twitter, Instagram, Facebook. The user base for so many of these applications was female, but the founders were men. Women weren't a part of the conversation. Less than 19 percent of the computer science graduates were women. I realized we needed to fill the gap. We needed to build that type of pipeline of talent. That's what inspired me to start Girls Who Code, to close the gender gap in technology jobs. I've built that organization over the past twelve years."

From Running for United States Congress to Founding Girls Who Code

Reshma's path shows us how a very public pivot was transformative to her life, the lives of many in the country, and around the world. From not winning the race for US Congress or New York City Public Advocate, these blows and involuntary pivots forced her forward on her path of purpose and glory.

She explains, "I joke that had I applied for CEO of Girls Who Code, I would never have gotten it. I didn't have the 'qualifications.' Even running for office, there weren't a lot of women; there still aren't a lot of women in politics who look like me, who have my background. Part of what I know I'm good at is building. I tell people, if you have an idea, instead of trying to go apply for that job, build it. I made up the rules as I went along. I found people who believed in me a little bit more than I believed in myself, such as former Secretary of State Hillary Clinton. I have always hired people who are smarter than me. I know what I need to build a team and a movement. The expertise I've built over the past fifteen years is in building movements and being able to communicate and translate complicated issues, whether it's girls in coding, or childcare, or paid leave, and I help get regular people to believe in it and fight for it."

Hijackings Can Be Upsetting. Protect Your Mental Health.

You may have noticed that our school, work, volunteer, and personal lives can be intense. There's so much competition, instability, fragility, rejection, and disappointment creating a pressure cooker. Everyone is concerned about holding on to their jobs and whatever possessions they have. These stressors only add to the mental health crisis we are currently facing.

To manage the inevitable mental and emotional toll, commit to taking good care of yourself. If this means being slower to figure out pivot plans, so be it. Rest and replenish. Invest in a therapist. Work on maintaining healthy relationships with those who positively pour into you. In short, keep yourself resilient and strong.

In the last chapter, I shared how I'd naively communicated my future goals with a boss who decided to punish me for aiming above her. It was traumatic. Those traumas aren't easy to forget, and they may take a long time—or a lifetime—to heal from. The gift of the experience, though, is the pattern recognition you gain. You'll be able to spot those enemy signals and avoid, deflect, and steer. You'll be less likely to doubt what you see, though others may gaslight you into believing that what you see and experience isn't real. Block them out. If for some reason you do miss the signs—we're human, it happens—the blow may hurt, but the recovery will be manageable because you have overcome and conquered pivots before, making you stronger and wiser. You will grow the armor to endure more redirection and be faster and nimbler in your pivots.

Make the Right Pivot at the Right Time

If you believe in God or forces in the universe or a higher power, know that many believe pivots are a divine redirection to that which is better for you. Regardless of what you believe, pivots and new directions take on the meaning that you give them.

Pivots can and should be empowering, not paralyzing, especially when they happen on your terms. Hijacks, though uncomfortable and sometimes downright painful, can prompt beneficial action and lead you to something even better than you have or imagined for yourself. CodeBreakers have the mindset, tools, resources, knowledge, and relationships to propel them forward.

The CodeBreaker Mindset™ Takeaways

- Build your pivot muscle continuously to buoy yourself and ride the waves of the agents of chaos, which will constantly try to engulf you.
- Be a collector and synthesizer of data and observations. Triangulation is elementary. Octagonulation gets into nth-dimensional chess and it's what the major players do. This skill will enable you to decode the nuanced data and signals telegraphing the enemy forces at play in the intersections of siege.
- Cross-reference the signs around you so you can get ahead of a possible takeover.
- If there's a lack of fundamental alignment with key stakeholders in your ecosystem, the substance does not match the form, and it is not solvable, then pivot to a better situation. If you don't, inevitably, the environment will eject you.
- When headwinds are irrational, you don't need to overanalyze their justification or legitimacy. Block out the noise and focus on problem-solving forward to a path of victory.

Chapter 7

Serendipity and Informed Intuition

> We cannot even imagine the complex forces behind every event that occurs in our lives. You never know how and when any life experience will reappear. You never know when a coincidence will lead to the opportunity of a lifetime.[24]
>
> —Dr. Deepak Chopra, award-winning author

The CodeBreaker Mindset™ Equation

[(Written Rules + Unwritten Rules) × Pivots] $^{\text{Serendipity, Informed Intuition}}$ =

Professional Judgment and Decision

Serendipity is a key ingredient in The CodeBreaker Mindset™ Equation. It can be a linear or nonlinear tailwind or headwind in your journey and a factor in anything you are pursuing. But what exactly is serendipity?

Most people answer something to the effect of being at the right place at the right time. That's true; timing is a critical piece of making a moment serendipitous.

Webster tells us serendipity is "the faculty or phenomenon of finding valuable or agreeable things not sought for."[25] But to be more comprehensive and tangible, I think of serendipity as the intersection and alignment of preparation, time, opportunity, energy, and intuition. At the intersection of these components are bursts of possibility and greatness. I know because it was a serendipitous event that opened the doors to my success.

Wall Street to TV

When I first entered journalism, I had no experience and knew no one in the field. I had a network of contacts built from my time in finance. Plus, I'd been told I had raw talent and drive that gave me what others described as "that spark." Broadcast journalism is what I was meant to do; that was clear to me and those around me. I knew if I didn't try to make a career of it, I would regret it for the rest of my life.

While reaching out to my network of contacts to try to get a foot in the journalism door, I contacted Jacque, a colleague and friend from when I had worked at Deutsche Bank. She suggested I speak with one of her acquaintances, Reggie. He wasn't in media but worked in consulting and knew a lot of people.

We set up a phone call, and during the conversation, I laid out my dream of being a business journalist. He listened, and I give him credit for never asking me, "Well, why would you want to leave your successful, well-paying career?" Instead, he said, "I know a few people. Let me make a phone call."

One of his contacts, a former TV news reporter, agreed to speak with me. I was in information-gathering mode, and she generously gifted me some gems on what was required to break into broadcast journalism. One of her timely suggestions was to attend the National Association of Black Journalists (NABJ) conference, which was happening in Philadelphia that year.

Generally speaking, there's not a lot of money in journalism. I was figuring out how to break into the business, and not earning much income at that point. I lived in New York City and, fortunately, could afford the train ticket for a short ride to Philadelphia. I didn't know anyone attending, and felt a bit intimidated at the prospect, but I told myself, *Just go check it out, meet people, and learn.* I have a mantra I live by that has served me well: If I don't go, how will I know? We have to put ourselves in the intersection and be open to the possible magnetism that may happen. So that's what I did.

It's true; serendipity is a magic chance encounter that leads to an opportunity beyond what you imagined. I'd like to suggest it's much more than simply timing. Let's dissect it at a granular level because once you understand the power of these moments and the benefit they'll have in your life—professionally and personally—you'll be analyzing every encounter you have from this lens and working to open yourself up to more of them.

Serendipity is a combination of the following five components:

1. Preparation
2. Timing
3. Opportunity
4. Energy
5. Intuition and Informed Intuition

Let's examine each component so we understand the role each one takes and how they build on each other.

Preparation

In chapter 4, I shared a quote by Roman philosopher Seneca who said, "Luck is what happens when preparation meets opportunity." While serendipity involves much more than this, preparation is the first critical component. Preparation is all the work you do to better situate yourself for those moments of intersection with people, places, and things, especially the key players you meet. You may have gotten your degree, but that job opportunity you're dreaming of won't just land in your lap while you wait for a response from the twenty potential employers to whom you sent your resume.

Being prepared involves knowing the written and unwritten rules. It means proactively thinking through how you want to present yourself. It's knowing how to communicate your ideas, especially in impromptu scenarios. Preparation is the embodiment of your life-to-date knowledge, skills, and visions of all that you hope to accomplish. Many people find it helpful to visualize what accomplishing that goal will look like.

People from the sports, media, and entertainment worlds have experienced remarkable success by using creative visualization. The list includes basketball icon LeBron James (four-time NBA Champion, NBA all-time leading scorer), swimming legend Katie Ledecky (nine-time Olympic gold medalist, twenty-one-time World Champion), media billionaire Oprah Winfrey, and music icon Katy Perry. US Olympian Lindsey Vonn, a highly decorated skier who won gold in downhill skiing in the 2010 Olympics, said, "I always visualize the [ski] run before I do it. By the time I get to the start gate, I've run the race 100 times already in my head, picturing how I'll take the turns. Once I visualize a course, I never forget it. So, I get on those lines and go through exactly the run that I want to have."[26] Have you visualized yourself winning your goal?

When the former TV news reporter suggested I attend the NABJ Conference in Philly, I intuitively knew it was a good idea. Preparation is about being ready for the moment when you're invited to enter the game. But to be clear, I'd never been to Philly before or taken that train. The conference was something I would have to pay for out of pocket, and money was tight. This created some level of doubt on whether I should go or not. It would have been easy for any doubt I felt to talk me out of going.

My dad used to say, "Time and tide wait for no man." In other words, "Carpe Diem" or "Seize the day!" The chance to attend NABJ in nearby

Philadelphia came to me unexpectedly. Whether I had other obligations or was feeling nervous about attending, I knew I had to push through. Preparation means sometimes pushing through how tired you are, how much else you have to do, or whatever constraints and doubts you are feeling, and going for it anyway.

I focused on my goal to succeed. It enabled me to reframe and see the signal that the universe was making it relatively easy to attend this conference. I figured out the budget to pay for the train ride and a one-day pass to the conference.

Prepare so you're ready when the stars align and you find yourself at the right place at the right time, and go for it! If you hesitate, you may miss out.

Timing

Timing is critical. When the timing is right, you may find yourself at the right physical or digital place to meet that right person or gain that right piece of information that adds, helps, or unlocks the potential of your pursuits.

When I signed up to attend the NABJ Conference, I was nervous. I love meeting people, and I knew it'd be informative, but I was in new territory. The whispers of doubt and negative words echoed in my head. But I couldn't deny that the stars were aligning. The conference was at the right time—I found out about it just in time to register. It was also in the right place—Philly was nearby, and I could afford and manage to travel there.

At the conference, I met many influential and highly regarded journalists. I also met a broadcasting icon, Soledad O'Brien. Meeting her would prove to be more than a little providential.

Think about all the times you've met a random person, and it ended up being someone who played a critical role in your life. You may have become good friends, or met someone related to a job opportunity, or someone who knows someone who knows someone at the company where you've always dreamed of working. Think about how you met your closest and lifelong friends. These serendipitous meetings happen because you found yourself in the right intersection at the right time. My friend Jacque put me in contact with people who knew people who made the conscious decision to help me.

Opportunity

The third element of serendipity is opportunity. Think of it as an opening. An opening for a job, to take a class, volunteer, meet a person, have a conversation, learn, or experience something. Imagine you're attending a job fair or conference and you catch word of a vacancy. No matter how prepared you are, you're looking for that opening. On the flip side, at that job fair, if you learn there's no opening for what you want to do, the conversation with the person is not wasted. There's still space for you to learn more about what skills that person and company are looking for, when there may be a career opening in the future, and to build a connection with that person. Opportunity is not only a binary outcome, such as an open seat for a job. It is also very important to have experiences with people, places, or things that make you informed, relevant, and equipped. Take an adventure that'll make for a great story that you can then use in a cover letter or put on your resume.

Opportunity is an opening where you can meet a key person, whether it's a famous leader or celebrity, a critical hiring manager, or someone who shares encouragement or information, which then prepares you for a future moment or thing.

Opportunity comes through people, places, and things.

Opportunity comes through experiences with people, places, and things.

Opportunity comes through information you observe and gather through your encounters with people, places, and things.

All the information and learning you gain from any opportunity informs your pattern recognition and intelligence of how you see, digest, and utilize all that comes your way, and how you subsequently choose to act.

Energy

Energy means feeling alignment or resonance, whether it's permanent or temporary, with the person to whom you're speaking. You're sending out positive vibes, and they're receiving them. The other person is also initiating or responding with positive, open vibes.

It doesn't have to be a deep encounter; the two of you just have to meet at a point of positive energy alignment, either in general or over something specific. I remember walking down the street in New York City, and Soledad O'Brien, who was a prominent, award-winning news anchor at CNN at the time, was approaching from the other direction. We made eye contact at the same time, both of us emanating a positive facial expression, and we each said hello.

Let me break this down. I was *prepared* in that I knew who she was, had remembered meeting her months prior at NABJ, and had the confidence to say hello and try to spark a conversation. That is *preparation*. On the *time* front, I was in the right place at the right time. I met her around 9:30 AM. I wasn't normally at that street intersection at that time, so it was the right place and right time. In terms of *opportunity*, I saw her in close proximity. There was an opening to say something—just a simple "Hello"—and then I was open to what unfolded. You help co-create what unfolds!

By the way, at the NABJ Conference where I had first met Soledad briefly, it hadn't been the optimal time to approach her; she was swamped with other attendees. I was able to say hello, but it wasn't the best time to engage her in an actual conversation. That morning on the street, I had a new moment present itself. After we both smiled and said hello, I introduced myself and launched into, "I met you before at the National Association of Black Journalists conference."

Mentioning NABJ meant something to her because she's a long-standing member. That enabled me to have some level of shared community with her, even if elementary in the moment, versus me being some random person approaching her. I then shared that I was a TV news journalist, and the conversation grew. We both were giving and receiving positive, open energy. Soledad was kind to engage with me. We exchanged contact info, and we organically discussed having a proper meeting. *Serendipity!* That encounter would subsequently prove to be critical to my career in broadcast journalism.

Now, this won't happen every time. We've all had the experience of meeting someone, and that person was closed off, and you end up feeling like you wasted your time. You're hurt that you went up to talk to them, but they weren't nice. You may feel rejected or a small knock to your confidence. Many people may brush you off because, like you, they're busy and preoccupied. They may not have the bandwidth in general, nor the bandwidth to be truly present in that moment to be open to spotting serendipity or opportunity. They may have been closed off or had blinders on. They may not like you for whatever reason, or think you are not important enough to speak with. Try not to take it personally. I know that's hard, as we've all been there. If you elevate yourself a bit, what it tells you is in that moment, there wasn't energy alignment. That's okay. There are more than eight billion people on the planet. You are not going to have energy alignment with all of them.

The power is in recognizing the lack of positive vibes and energy alignment and allowing it to teach you a data point about that person that you can add to your pattern recognition, either on them specifically or on such encounters in general. Then, exit the exchange and move on. Keep it moving to glide yourself to the next beautiful encounter that inevitably awaits you.

It's serendipity to come prepared, be in the right place at the right time, be open to recognizing opportunity, and to have mutual positive energy and resonance with the person you are trying to engage.

Intuition and Informed Intuition

Raw Intuition

The final element necessary for serendipity is intuition, and as you have experience and pattern recognition, this becomes informed intuition.

According to *Psychology Today*, "Intuition is the ability to understand something instinctively, without any need for conscious reasoning or an explanation. The use of intuition is sometimes referred to as responding to a 'gut feeling' or 'trusting your gut.'"[27] Intuition, at its root, is your raw gut telling you to proceed or not to proceed. To talk to that person or not to talk to that person. To make that right turn or stay straight. To take a step forward or not. To take the shot or not. For example, have you ever found yourself trying to park a car, and no spaces are available? You don't want to pay a high fee, so you decide to head down a side street, and boom, there's a spot. What led you one way instead of another? Intuition.

Informed Intuition = Raw Intuition + Pattern Recognition

The intuition we relied on as children or young adults was instinctive, raw, and innately informed. *Psychology Today* also states that "Intuition relies on evolutionarily older, automatic, unconscious, and fast mental processing, primarily to save our brains time or energy."[28]

As we get older and gain more experience, we learn to recognize when our intuition is speaking to us. We are more proficient because we know what intuition is and how it can help us. *Psychology Today* goes on to say, "Intuition later in life arises from the accumulation of knowledge and experiences that are processed and stored in our brain's neural networks, as well as other cells and tissues in our bodies, allowing us to access this information quickly, often unconsciously.

"Intuition is at the core of an epiphany; it is our own recognition and awareness of an idea or thought or vision for something that has yet to be discovered in the world. We all have access to that place if we only learn to trust that internal voice."[29] Our life-to-date knowledge and experiences are what create, inform, and develop our pattern recognition, and the outcome of that raw intuition + pattern recognition over time is what I refer to as informed intuition.

To bring this to life, let's go back to when we were babies. We learned to sit up, crawl, stand, and walk. Inevitably, there was natural trial and error. We would hurt ourselves and then get back up. The adults in our lives helped us crawl, walk, and run. A lot of that came to us intuitively, and even as a baby, we developed early pattern recognition from what felt good and bad, such as falling. We forged ahead, relying on our earliest existence of informed intuition on how to crawl, stand, and walk more stably. In a discussion forum on "*biology*," participants exchanged ideas on "What motivates children to start walking?" A member said, "When we first start walking, usually we fail many times but still we have this natural motivation [to] learn walking despite the failure. Is this some sort [of] 'intuitive' intelligence which babies have? To be more specific, I can't imagine a baby to consider the pros and cons of walking vs. crawling and then logically argue to himself/herself that learning how to walk would be something worthwhile to spend his [her] mental resources on."[30]

Over time, intuition isn't just raw intuition. It becomes informed intuition. Your gut told you to walk as a baby. After multiple attempts at walking, your mind and body responded to a pattern recognition that developed and sharpened over time, enabling you to walk. You may see parallels here with learning to ride a bike, swim, or skate.

Informed intuition is the moment you realize serendipity is happening. Picking up on meeting Soledad O'Brien, when I saw her near Central Park in New York City with an opening to say hello, I knew serendipity was in motion. After that encounter, Soledad and I had our follow-up meeting, and many more meetings. She ended up taking me under her wing and mentoring me as I was new to the TV journalism industry. Soledad broke down the written and unwritten rules. She told me about the inevitable pivots. The knowledge, resources, and support she gifted me were invaluable. This was not only serendipity but a tailwind force that accelerated my learning curve and ability to navigate the thorny media industry.

You may think that I was just super lucky to meet Soledad and have her as a mentor, as she didn't have to show me such kindness and generosity. But it was more than luck. I had a role to play in every moment and interaction with her. What if I had not been prepared for our impromptu encounter on that Manhattan street corner? What if I felt doubt or couldn't find the words, and did not open my mouth and speak?

Preparation, timing, opportunity, energy, informed intuition—these are the five elements that were present, aligned, and realized to result in serendipity.

Missing the Magic

What if you miss the moment of serendipity? You couldn't see it for whatever reason. Sometimes, the universe gives you an opportunity, an opening, or energy with someone, but you're not able to identify it because you are expecting it to come in a different way or form.

We can't get it right every single time. It's just not realistic. We will have times when we miss a signal. I learned this a long time ago because I'd miss a golden opportunity and then, afterward, kick myself. I'd be licking my wounds, feeling disappointed in myself. I eventually realized it was a learning opportunity to be aware, recognize, prepare, and build the muscle memory for the next time. There are instances where not getting or missing that chance opens the door for something else.

Maybe you wanted to go to a particular school, but you didn't get in. Instead, you're accepted to your second choice, which is still a good school, so you go. Or you interview for one job, then find out it's filled, but they offer you another position.

In our minds, we have a certain idea, person, place, thing, experience, or outcome visualized, whether we admit it or not. Often, the universe, existence, or life sends us something else. It may not be what we expected, but it leads us down a path that may often be better than we imagined. It goes back to the saying that you cannot connect the dots of your life forward; you can only connect them backward.

Let's say you come out of a coffee shop on a Saturday morning, and as you're walking down the sidewalk, the hiring manager of a company you'd like to join is walking in the opposite direction. Never in a million years did you expect to see them there! You kept walking, and now you're kicking yourself because you missed your moment.

This happens to all of us. But at the risk of putting a bit of pressure on you, how else could this have gone? Did you just derail or miss the serendipity train? Maybe. But there isn't only one instance of serendipity. Opportunities appear all the time. Serendipity is also the moment you realize you passed that person, but while you're banging your open palm against your forehead, someone else knocks into you and says, "Oh, excuse me." And it's another new person and opportunity filled with possibility.

You think your future opportunity will show up a certain way at a certain time, but it often comes in a form and at a time you didn't expect. Don't fixate too much on it being exactly as you visualized it for years. Spot the substance over the binary, fixed form. Leave room for the universe to look out for you and send something else that is new, better, and enriching.

Professional Judgment and Decision

Each one of us is in pursuit of something, whether opportunity, knowledge, work, relationships, or experience. Now that you have a more complete understanding of The CodeBreaker Mindset™ Equation, you're positioned to use the inputs and methodologies to achieve your desired outcome.

Enjoy using the equation to strengthen your ability to make sound professional judgments. The more you use it, the quicker you'll adapt to the good, bad, and neutral situations that come your way. You won't be caught off guard when headwinds swirl around you because you'll be two steps ahead.

We may be born CodeBreakers with infinite wisdom and intuition living within us. The opportunity is to access these resources and manifest the possibilities. Irrespective of being born with it, we become CodeBreakers as we learn and grow our knowledge, skills, and expertise to combat the headwinds and capitalize on the tailwinds.

Insights from Leaders on Serendipity and Informed Intuition

CASE STUDY

Dr. Astro Teller, The Moonshot Factory (division of Alphabet), Co-Founder and Captain

"I think of intuition as just pattern matching. Or if you think of it like we have these little production rules in our head, A implies B, B implies C, C implies D. At some point, we've seen that so many times that we know that A implies D because of the chain rule of those implications.

"I think the moments of intuition are really that kind of pattern matching, where we've just learned enough rules, we've practiced them enough that we no longer are doing it at a conscious level. Some of it is happening unconsciously, but that doesn't mean our brain isn't sorting through these kinds of implications in our lives.

"Serendipity is pretty critical for what we're doing. It's a lot of where our raw material comes from. But we can't just be like wild and crazy and trying anything, any time. Then it would just be a mess here with no focus or direction. A lot of what's challenging about making a Moonshot Factory is how do you allow for a lot of nonconformity, a lot of serendipity and creativity and exploration, but also kind of shape and focus it so that it doesn't kill the creativity, but it also doesn't allow the creativity to be formless."

CASE STUDY

Tory Burch, Tory Burch LLC, Founder, Executive Chairman, Chief Creative Officer

"I think you can create your own luck and serendipity. From a young age, my parents told me, 'Negativity is noise.' They taught me to be an optimist, to believe in myself, and to surround myself with people who would do the same. The greatest example of serendipity may have been meeting my husband, Pierre-Yves [Roussel] . . . who is now my CEO. I was the creative director and CEO for fourteen years, and it became increasingly tough. As our business grew, I was being pulled in a million directions, and I had less and less time for what I really loved: design. I knew I needed to refine my role, and I spent years looking for the right person to take over my operating role. That turned out to be Pierre-Yves, who had been the CEO of LVMH Fashion Group for fifteen years. It was the best—and easiest—decision I've ever made. We complement each other and are fundamentally aligned. I feel incredibly lucky to have him as a partner."

CASE STUDY

Jon Korngold, Blackstone, Global Head of Blackstone Growth

"To the extent that you feel that you are in control of your destiny, I think that's such a fool's errand. There's so much more around you that is outside of your control. I'll give you an example. I met my wife on the Crosstown bus on three serendipitous encounters. She was running late, which never happens, and I was running early, which doesn't happen. I'm never late, but I always say that being almost late is right on time. It was my very first day at work, actually, coming out of business school, and I met her, and my life changed because of that. I wasn't supposed to be back in New York until the following week, but ended up coming home earlier and found an apartment that was across the street from her."

CASE STUDY

Navin Chaddha, Mayfield Fund, Managing Partner

"I think serendipity is very important. I believe everybody works hard who's trying to be an entrepreneur. We always have the right people who are trying to do good things with the right values. Two things have to happen. You need to be in the right place. My case, Silicon Valley. Here, center of innovation when I did my first company. The next thing is right time. When the confluence of right people, right place, right time happens, magic happens. That has happened to me not once, [but] multiple times.

"It's happening again with AI, right? There are very few people in the venture capital business in early stage who have been through cycles since the mid-nineties. I'm lucky that I'm one of them and have enough pattern recognition. On intuition, at the early investing stage, when you're starting a company, first principles win. Don't overthink."

CASE STUDY

Ndidi Okonkwo Nwuneli, ONE Campaign, President and CEO

"The simplest definition of intuition is that you don't make decisions based on rational thoughts or data. You make it from another part of your brain that is linked to mental models of previous experiences. Mental models of a gut check don't feel right. Mental models linked to a feeling and experience of thoughts that, on paper, looking at the data might not be justified by that data, nor the rational side of your brain, but just give you a sense that there's something going on here. Some people call it a gut feeling.

"Serendipity for me is almost like the combination of chance, luck. It's quite different in my view from intuition. Was it serendipity that I met Chitra at a dinner and happened to sit next to her? Or was it divine intervention? I don't know. But how we leverage that conversation to then make a decision to connect was intuition as opposed to serendipity. You leverage those chance encounters, those special, magical moments, to then determine how they shape your life. I think that's where intuition comes in."

CASE STUDY

Reshma Saujani, Girls Who Code and Moms First, Founder

"I think everything happens for a reason. I think we all end up exactly where we're supposed to end up. Had I not lost that congressional race, I never would have started Girls Who Code. Had I not lost my public advocate race, I would have never built Girls Who Code. Had I not had ten years of fertility challenges, had my son not been born exactly on January 25, 2020, in the pandemic, I never would have started Moms First. I wouldn't have been a mom trying to raise a newborn in a pandemic while homeschooling my five-year-old. I wouldn't have been at that moment where it would have been so much that I would have seen something that I had never seen before."

In the next section, we'll look at the attitudes, behaviors, and calculated actions that build The CodeBreaker Mindset™. This includes the rules of information gathering, how to read the room, connect the dots, build strong relationships, and pilot the missiles of difficult personalities.

The CodeBreaker Mindset™ Takeaways

- Recognize that serendipity is both linear and nonlinear. It's both a tailwind and a headwind. Optimal alignment of preparation, time, opportunity, energy, and informed intuition has the potential to be a tailwind, driving positive nonlinear outcomes.
- Have a mental, physical, or digital cheat sheet to recognize the elements of preparation, time, opportunity, energy alignment, and informed intuition.
- Informed Intuition = Raw Intuition + Pattern Recognition.
- Recognize there's always value in taking the shot as you're learning and building muscle memory. There is no such thing as perfect. The more you take the shot, the more you will learn and master how to act on serendipity, and how to optimize intersecting with a person, place, thing, or experience.
- Just like with the concept of return on investment (ROI), optimize your return on intersection.

PART II

Become A CodeBreaker

Chapter 8

Information Is Power

> When the facts change, I change my mind. What do you do, sir?[31]
>
> —John Maynard Keynes, renowned economist

Do you sense the transformation happening as your mindset shifts toward CodeBreaking? You're growing more aware of the invisible movements bouncing between people—whether it's thoughts, emotions, energy, or nuances. You're picking up on the subtext of their words and actions, as well as explicit and hidden meanings behind how things get done. This gives you the opportunity to form an armor of protection against being unsuspecting, clueless, and caught unaware. You are building muscles you never knew you had.

Critical to building The CodeBreaker Mindset™ is the completeness of inputs and information that inform and power The CodeBreaker Mindset™ Equation. These two words, inform and information, are the roots of everything in life. In this chapter, we'll discuss the different kinds of information to understand how to interpret and use them as armor and an advantage.

In chapter 1, we explored how any goal or dream involves playing a game. Now I will reveal something that will give you an edge, regardless of your industry: The winner is the person who has access to the most complete and diverse information set. Homogeneity won't help. Gathering as much information from the most holistic fact set, then analyzing, triangulating, and octogonulating that information will enable you to invent the best ideas and methodology of action.

Octogonulating

Is this word new for you? Let's sidebar on this for a moment. Triangulation, according to Webster, is a calculation or prediction based on known facts.[32]

Triangulation is a term used when approaching and analyzing a situation from three angles to get the full picture and think through possible outcomes. Octogonulating is triangulating multiplied by eight angles. But not only eight angles, as many as you can get your hands on, and as many as necessary. It is about finding, analyzing, and synthesizing as many data points as you can in order to get the whole picture of a situation. It's seeing patterns or non-patterns that others can't, knowing what others don't. The treasure is in original insights, ideas, and intellectual property (IP).

How often does a unique insight or original idea happen? The race and chase are for the information leading to the insight that others cannot find, or are not as fast as you in discovering. Part of the tech war is using AI to outrun rivals to reach these gems.

Is the Information Any Good?

Information comes from many sources. One way we gain information is by receiving feedback from others. Unfortunately, the world is filled with people who, for a variety of reasons, have their own agendas, priorities, and biases. They have their own frames of reference and lenses through which they see the world and determine what they value.

It's hard to find common denominators of shared values with people, as we talked about in the agents of chaos. Thus, when people give feedback, it may be to serve us, be random and aimless, or not have our best interests at heart. Often, unless the giver of the input is cognizant, they may give feedback that serves them before it serves us, if it ever serves us at all.

The usefulness of any piece of information depends on evaluating the integrity and efficacy of the source, and then on what we do with it. Critical to its effectiveness is our ability to analyze and classify what others tell us because it impacts our confidence and, in many cases, directly determines what we choose. However, as with most things, the quality of the output, and therefore the quality of the analysis, is only as good as the quality of the input.

Tech and AI, especially AI, are only as good as the data we feed them. The inputs must be high quality and holistic. The best AI is a function of the inputs and the quality of the actual algorithm. Your information gathering starts with seeking out diverse sources of data, not just popular opinion.

The quality of the input also needs to be as independent and objective as possible. Here is where diversity and different sources of information come in. If you input biased data, when it is analyzed and processed through the "black box," the response it spits out is skewed. How then can you make the best decision, whether it's what school to send your child to, how to scale your business, the best way to pivot, or how to find your purpose? The best outcome requires the best analysis, but before the analysis, you've got to have the most optimal inputs.

Furthermore, all types and sources of information are not equal. Are you always careful to filter who and what you listen to? As much as you love your best friend, they may not be the best person to counsel you on all matters. Question and verify the authenticity and integrity of the input source. How much weight do you give to each source of input? These are critical determinants that can make or break you.

Three Types of Information

We are taught to seek feedback and listen to other people's perspectives. What we're generally not taught is how to examine the feedback we're given and the motives of the person offering it.

Feedback shapes us from a young age. Consider how positive or negative feedback affects a baby, child, teenager, or adult of any age. Positive feedback can propel us and build up our confidence, while negative feedback can chip away at our mental and emotional well-being in conscious and subconscious ways. Skewed and false feedback hurt our self-preparedness and ability to fortify and equip ourselves with whatever attributes and tools are needed to succeed.

Seek out as many different sources as possible. Vet and synthesize those sources to know what is fact versus distortion. Think back to the agents of chaos and our discussion on social media. Not everything you read can be trusted. In information gathering, you also need to consider the intention of the person, company, network, or voice providing it. Is their intention to gift you with data-driven, perception-driven, or manipulation-driven information?

Data-Driven Information

Data-driven information is the best and closest thing to the truth. The closer you are to understanding the truth of a given situation, the better decisions you will make—whether it is decisions about how you adjust and calibrate your thoughts, words, feelings, or actions, or how those decisions impact your engagement with the people around you.

Data-driven information is independently objective, verifiable, and often quantifiable. It can be corroborated, substantiated, and supported with tangible evidence. For example, the population of the United States is close to 335 million. This can be verified with the US Census Bureau, as well as federal and state websites. When parsing the authenticity of the data, ask yourself: Do multiple sources provide the same facts?

The following are some techniques to help you decode the level of facts and objectivity in what others tell you.

Relational Feedback

Information and feedback being given on people by other people is relational feedback. This is tricky because it's difficult to apply a scientific method to validate if the feedback and its giver are objective.

Have you heard of the phrase "beauty is in the eyes of the beholder"? This is the most analogous to demonstrating what relational feedback looks like. Using beauty as an example, can you provide a global, unifying, singular definition and benchmark of beauty? One person may give feedback that something is beautiful, whereas another person, country, or culture may not. Thus, the feedback on whether something is beautiful is relational and relative to the underlying contexts, assumptions, and standards. Compare and contrast this to passing a math test, where you have to answer the questions accurately. Math is binary in that $1 + 1 = 2$. If you answer the question correctly, then you pass the test. You can give feedback that someone is good at math if they get the answers correct more times than not.

Substance Matches the Form

Does the substance of the information match the form? For example, we are often called to give a job reference. There are situations when a person is given as a reference but has never actually worked with the person, whether as an employee, client, vendor, or other stakeholder. Substance versus form here means a job reference coming from a person who has substantively worked with you and the nature of the work being characterized. We'll have fun with an example of this later in the chapter.

Firsthand Data and Experience

The person giving the feedback has had substantive, direct interactions with you—ideally multiple interactions with you over a number of scenarios, contexts, and years.

Wide Range of Data and Experience

The person giving the advice has seen you firsthand in a wide breadth and depth of situations. They've been with you in multiple scenarios and have seen you at your best, worst, and in between.

Intentional and Thoughtful

The person has had the time to be thoughtful and formulate an assessment after compiling and compounding a series of direct interactions with you in various scenarios.

Rooted in Empathy

The person offering you feedback understands who you are. Or they take the time to understand who you are, your context, and to receive you as closely as possible to your intentions. They are in your corner, looking to help you become a better person, accentuate your strengths, and help you advance your goals. This kind of feedback, unfortunately, is rare.

Does the Feedback Feel Like a Tailwind?

Following on the last point, the feedback should feel like a tailwind. The input is designed and delivered in a way to propel you forward. Note, we don't mean folks who tell you what you want to hear and "yes" you to life. Real, legitimate tailwind feedback is always welcome, not reverse gaslighting. The feedback is given using a communication approach that resonates with you. It's given in a way that helps you understand and problem solve the gaps.

Pattern of Feedback Emerging from Multiple Sources

You receive similar feedback from multiple people and sources and can see a pattern in the feedback to conclude on plausibility and validity.

Data Is Nothing Without Interpretation

Another dimension of data-driven input is that, in many cases, the data does not tell you by itself how to interpret it. There is a propensity to think that it does, and this is especially true of quantitative output. Back to arithmetic for a moment, 1 + 1 = 2. Is two always good? Two problems are not better than one problem. However, two glasses of water to drink are generally better than one. Thus, another critical dimension of data-driven intel is the lens the giver and receiver use to interpret the results. That lens is based on many factors such as geography, culture, socio-economic status, demographics, etc. Be aware of the context and interpretation that a magnifying glass can apply to the data.

Looking at ChatGPT in the context of data-driven feedback, is it data-driven, or is there ambiguity? Many experts contend that ChatGPT is data-driven, but it isn't. ChatGPT is programmed by many people, and while they may not be intentionally perception- or manipulation-driven, they may be inputting data based on their perception and interpretation of the material. This is how any AI algorithm is programmed. The data will include pure input + context + some level of interpretation. That interpretation is a function of their conscious and subconscious knowledge, awareness, and bias, as well as their perception, frame of reference, experience, etc.

I'm not saying Dr. Evil is behind AI and manipulating us, but I'm not saying that it's impossible either.

Perception-Driven Information

Perception is based on several things, including a person's conscious and subconscious biases, interpretations, frames of reference, and insecurities. Perception is how you read, digest, interpret, process, and spew information back to others.

The person giving the information may not be objective. Like all of us, they have their own life experiences and way of viewing the world. They have their own physical, mental, spiritual, and emotional triggers, pain, and heartache, so they may provide you with information slanted from their perception. Understand that this happens all the time, especially in the working world, and it's not something we can control.

Perception-driven information and feedback can damage your physical, mental, emotional, and spiritual well-being. It can hurt your mindset. This can then stunt how you view and love yourself, how you feel, and how you act. Worrying about what other people think of you entices you to succumb to the status quo rather than being an independent thinker and doer.

Promotion Based on Perception

When I worked in investment banking, I was on a management committee of a division that was charged with voting on the promotions of colleagues in different regions. A candidate from Japan was up for promotion, and the majority of us, all but one person, had never met the individual nor worked with him directly. Voting was based on second- and third-hand information, on hearsay or "perception-say."

The majority of my male colleagues (I was the only female) on the committee voted for the man not to be promoted.

I was incensed by the lack of professionalism and methodology. Shame on that management group, the human resources department, and the process. How could the majority of the management team vote on a man they had never met? How could one accurately assess if the candidate had fulfilled the promotion requirements, which in this case were leadership-oriented in nature, and thus weighted more subjectively over production metrics?

Furthermore, we live in an age where you can meet and interact with anyone digitally, so the physical location of the man in Asia was not a sufficient barrier. Instead of doing the legwork to make an informed decision, it was easier to just say that the colleague in Japan was not ready for this new role. Secretly, many in the group wanted to promote another candidate.

When it came my turn to vote, I declined, saying I had insufficient information. I am not trying to prop myself up here, but how many people step out and say, "Sorry, I am not going to vote on perception-say or hearsay"?

Substantive experience is data-driven. If it is not substantive, it is not data-driven, and it should have no place because it isn't reliable. It's astonishing how many decisions get made based solely on perception. Why?

Skimming for Ease

Laziness. Skimming through life looking for the path of least resistance. Not being incentivized. Not having the desire, energy, or bandwidth to invest the time to sift through to the data. Wanting the easy answer, the answer that you can handle, or that serves your agenda.

There is a side to human nature where many like to gossip rather than take the time to investigate, get the facts, and assess. There can be an inclination, and some level of instant gratification, to churn the rumor mill rather than meet the person, ask questions, and understand why they operate the way they do. With the agents of chaos, people have even less time, patience, and bandwidth to do this work, but the work still needs to be done if we intend to uphold integrity.

If you find yourself getting advice from a person who seems glued to supporting and perpetuating perception-driven information, they are not your friend. For that person, it isn't about merit. Irrespective of whether they are well-intentioned or not, if the person is not willing to parse out data-driven versus perception-driven information, then they are taking a shortcut. They may be prioritizing what's the easy answer for them, their agenda, or what serves them best.

Perception Is a Cop-Out

Perception-driven information is a cop-out. With all the tools, tech, and AI we have available at our fingertips, we should have the bandwidth to stop perception-driven decisions, but instead, we feed the beast of mediocrity. We can all do better, especially in the workplace and as information givers. We tell ourselves we don't have the time to do the work, but then we spend half an hour scrolling Instagram. Or we escape into a video game or stream some show on Netflix while riding the train to and from work. Why not take thirty minutes to make a phone call to investigate and get the data on a person, situation, or scenario?

Perception Can Be a Crime

One of the biggest crimes committed against people in the workplace is how decisions about pay, promotion, opportunity, and career movement are made based on perception rather than direct, substantive experience with that person.

A person in this scenario should have the maturity to say, "I cannot give feedback on this person because I do not know them." Instead, we give feedback because it feels good to be asked, it makes us feel important, or because we want to weigh in. It's human nature to want to speak about others, especially if we have something negative to share. It's a form of being trigger-happy. It takes self-discipline to stop oneself and say, "Hey, I can't give input because I don't have enough information."

Often, what happens when a person does not have the data is they recycle feedback, and parrot or paraphrase hearsay or material they overheard from others. By piling on more feedback, they feel important and in the know. This feedback may have been given by someone who is mired in their own junk, is insecure, or has a scarcity mindset. They may believe things about you that aren't true but that are grounded in their baggage and perceptions. If a person does not like you for whatever reason, they may be less incentivized to do the work and get the data, and happily live in their perceptions and misperceptions about you. While they may not be seeking to actively hurt you, they're not trying to help you either.

Expecting Others to Be the Same

Another aspect of perception includes an expectation that others should behave, talk, think, feel, and speak like us. If they don't, then there is more room for the input giver to interpret or misinterpret, skewing how they give feedback. Let's say I am interviewing candidates for a job that requires interpersonal skills, and a candidate comes across as introverted or self-identifies that way. I may cast that person out because I perceive they will not have the interpersonal skills to do the job. Or I may make a subconscious, automatic assessment that the person is introverted, and they are quiet and not sociable. It's so much easier to judge a book by its cover. Our judgment of a person is often formed by how similar or different they appear and feel to us.

If we slow down, do some checking, and ask questions, we might realize that while this person might think and speak a bit differently, they may still be able to get the job done. The point is to focus on the substance, not the form. It's not how the person appears. It's how they perform. In this example, this is demonstrated by their values, thought process, communication, and operating approach.

Don't Be Fooled by Form

The world is being fooled by form. They think if it looks like a duck, it must be a duck. Don't get caught up in the surface level, shiny, or sexy. If you don't understand the substance, all you have to offer is perception-driven information and feedback, which helps no one.

The challenge and opportunity are to go against the grain of accepting and operating in mediocrity and perception, and instead, deal in cold, hard truth. People like perception because it serves some master. Many don't like the truth because the real truth has no master. So those who love perception don't want to be at the mercy of truth.

Manipulation-Driven Information

Manipulation-driven information is feedback that isn't objective. It is targeted and calculated, based on an outcome the other person is trying to achieve. People who give this kind of information tend to be very sophisticated, and they're about trickery and treachery. They're doing this to drive specific outcomes.

In many environments, especially business and political, feedback contains elements that are manipulation-driven. These people are playing four-, eight-, or n-dimensional chess. The feedback may be data-driven, based on perception, or neither. However, the person giving the feedback is using any ingredients they have to cook up the outcome they want. They will say and do whatever it takes, however explicit or subtle.

Here are some attributes that point to manipulation-driven information and feedback at play:

- Lack of transparency
- Lack of a fair, free, and competitive marketplace
- Actors in the ecosystem have an undue power concentration or unfair competitive advantage
- Lack of checks and balances, regulation, law, and controls
- Information disintermediation and fragmentation
- Cultural, social, and accepted norms of manipulation
- Vague, ambiguous, or opaque answers when trying to verify and substantiate information and feedback

Let's reflect on this in the context of influencers and social media. Many influencers have well-curated and coiffed photos in their social media feed, portraying a certain narrative, projecting an orchestrated vision they want you to have of them. This may be to attract brands that pay them for endorsements and to use their products and services in the social sphere. The value here is intangible and can be transient and transactional. Social media users and followers may not realize the influencer is being paid, and erroneously think the product association is authentic, motivating them to buy the product.

Manipulating the Numbers

Venture capital is another example where intentional influence and orchestration to drive outcomes occur frequently. There are many early stage companies where it's too soon to know if the technology, product, service, or market opportunity is truly viable, yet millions and billions of dollars are invested, which drives valuations to astronomical levels. The founder/entrepreneur, who may have invested their life savings in the business, will craft narratives, along with the venture capitalist, to woo stakeholders into believing the vision and business model, in order to get buy-in on the actual or perceived high valuations.

In companies of any size and scale, what the market and stakeholders value may change in a moment and continue evolving over many years. Thus, manipulation narratives are also a function of a spinning roulette wheel of changes in business, life, and people. The proprietor or investor may calibrate information and feedback loops because the desired outcomes are dynamic and fluid. They may see if there are data-driven or perception-driven mechanisms, or both, that they can use or twist to drive the results they seek. The twisting leads to manipulation-driven mechanisms.

This happens everywhere, but I have observed it happen the most in contexts where the risks and stakes are high, and so much of the value is intangible, ambiguous, and based on perception—and orchestrating perception. You could also be operating in an intersection where business and assets are illiquid, and it's hard to get independent verification of parameters, transactions, and economic values. It is in these situations where manipulation likely exists. The agents of chaos amplify all these dynamics even more.

When value is formed, it is contingent on relativity that drives the value up or down, and you will see a higher propensity of manipulation-driven information and feedback when value is intangible. Imagine you discover a diamond. We all know what a diamond is. An independent appraiser can value the diamond to determine its worth, based on carat, cut, color, and other specifications. This evaluation has a tangible value. It can be quantified and independently verified. The more intangible or ambiguous something is, the more that value is relational and created based on perception, ambiguity, transient form, and relativity—artificial, not substantive. The owner or beneficiaries of that asset will want to maintain and maximize its value.

In the startup example, if I am a founder, I don't want to lose the value of my company, and potentially most of my net worth, so I'll say anything to get the outcome I want. The information and feedback are driven by my agenda and need to control the outcome. I'm trying to maintain my position, power, and influence. A large part of manipulation-driven information is about having control. The giver of the information wants to control the chess game—from who plays, how the moves are made, the order, sequence, and, ultimately, the outcome.

Fear of Missing Out (FOMO)

In some industries, such as venture capital, FOMO is an intentional mechanism—perception- and manipulation-based—to drive fear and actions.

CASE STUDY

Steve Kraus, Bessemer Venture Partners, Partner

Venture capitalist Steve Kraus, a partner at multi-billion-dollar Bessemer Venture Partners (BVP), is no stranger to this as he has ridden the investing roller coaster for twenty-plus years.

BVP isn't only one of the most preeminent investors in the world, it's the oldest venture capital firm, starting in 1911 as the family office of Henry Phipps. Mr. Phipps was once a partner with Andrew Carnegie, the great American industrialist who founded Carnegie Steel, which ultimately was sold to U.S. Steel. Steve has invested in more than fifty companies, several of which have had multi-million- to billion-dollar exits and gone public, such as Allscripts and Collective Medical.

Steve educated me on what sources of information he uses to make investment decisions, including how he triangulates data and looks for non-consensus, as well as how he's conscious not to be sucked in by FOMO. Steve says, "I pay attention to what other venture capitalists do, but I don't use that as a signal because I think there's a lot of FOMO in our industry. There's so many great spaces and entrepreneurs to invest in. I don't lose sleep at night about that, which is weird. Some people are very in tune with what deals we miss. Yes, I don't like to miss investments and opportunities, but I don't let what other venture capitalists do drive my decision-making."

Find Spaces That Are Non-Consensus

Steve emphasizes finding spaces that are non-consensus. He says, "When it becomes consensus, when every single other investor is looking at that space, all of a sudden, prices for the assets and companies that you're interested in go up because investing is a law of supply and demand. If there's more demand for your company, you'll be able to raise at higher valuations.

You can invest $5 million at a $20 million valuation, or you can invest $5 million at a $200 million valuation. The more non-consensus, and the earlier you find something, the better the opportunity. You're going to be able to invest the money and own a lot more of that company."

Keenly looking for patterns of non-consensus to guide investing is beautifully analogous to the benefits of studying outliers, which we delve into in chapter 12.

Triangulate the Data

BVP highlights its data-driven approach even when the verifiable internal and external data vary in maturity from early stage to growth stage to late stage companies. Steve asserts, "At the early stages, the information you're getting is external data on the opportunity because there might not be financial data when the entrepreneur comes and presents to you. They might not have an income statement or customers. There's data in the product. You can go talk to potential customers as data. Try to take that external data and jam it against what the entrepreneur is working on and triangulate if there's an opportunity. Founders sharing their background, strengths, weaknesses, what they think the pitfalls might be . . . that's all data.

"Later-stage companies have more financial data. We spend a lot of time understanding how these companies grow and mature and what the metrics should look like. In the early stage, you've got to play a different game than the late stage and the growth stage. Then there's the malfeasance side. I've looked at some of the companies in our space that ultimately were colossal failures and maybe even engaged in some senses of fraud." Thus obtaining data-driven information to support assessments is crucial.

A Story Can't Tell the Data

Steve also asserts, "Once you get into more mature companies, the picture becomes clear when you look at the data. One of my partners always says,

'The data can tell a story. A story can't tell the data.' Not everyone's perfect all the time, and some people sell ahead of things. But if you notice several instances where the data doesn't match up with the story they're telling, usually those are yellow flags as well."

The choice is clear. Stick with data-driven information as much as you can. Steer away from information that is based on perception or manipulation. Realize there is no foolproof way to avoid it, but your odds of sniffing out tainted information are higher when you pause and analyze the content, look at it from all angles, and remain ahead of your opponent.

Learn to Play the Game

Those who give manipulation-driven information may be annoyed that I'm sharing this intel. They would much rather the population be oblivious to the inner workings of the highest echelons of power and influence. Realize that anyone who wants to keep you in the dark is not your friend. Those are not the people you want to have substantive dealings with. If you sense this shadiness and still choose to proceed, do so at your own risk and beware.

Know how to play the information game. Here's a practical example. Imagine you're in a meeting and you realize the manager is giving manipulation-driven information. How do you respond? Play the game to stay in the game? Be ready with a counter move? Come prepared with data? Maybe it means having a meeting with a key colleague beforehand and giving them a heads up, "Hey, Tom is about to slam you on some issues. But he doesn't have the data. I've got the data to counter and shut down his perception-driven and manipulation-driven attacks."

A key part of The CodeBreaker Mindset™ is knowing what is happening, what you're up against, and getting ahead of it, or at least knowing how to deal with it in real time. Try not to be paralyzed or permanently stuck.

For example, if a future employer asks, "If I were to call your manager Tom for a reference, what would he say?" My response would be, "He doesn't want you to hire me because you're the company's biggest competitor. So he'll tell you I didn't deliver, even though I did. Feel free to call him. Let me also give you four customer references to add perspective."

It's all a game of chess. It's about strategy and knowing how to use information to your advantage or to neutralize false, non-data-driven information and negativity. I'm not saying be a perpetrator of manipulation-driven information, nor a bad actor. Become smarter at how to use data to neutralize, combat, or shut down the negative perception and manipulation headwinds.

Most People Don't Give Effective Feedback

Most people are not capable, proficient, or even trained in how to give effective feedback. Be careful who you go to for counsel. Will going to those ill-equipped to give proper feedback help or harm you? Are you willing to take the risk to get the information, even if it may be delivered sub-optimally? Will you do the work to parse through the input and repurpose it to get the nuggets of wisdom that can help you? When a person is not about themselves, they can be about data. Think about that. If a person really wants to offer helpful information, they'll gift input that will move you forward.

It's human nature for people to provide feedback anchored in the way that they see the world, situation, and context. This means that wired into their thinking and communicating is their personal dictionary and baseline filled with their frames of reference, standards, and values. Thus, they may give you input based on what they think is good for you, not necessarily what is good for you based on your identity, constitution, standards, and values. Ask yourself, is the person guiding you based on what they think you should be and do? Or are they advising you based on your definition of who you are, who you want to be, and what you want to do?

When I was in high school, I investigated joining the Armed Forces and attending the Royal Military College of Canada. I had a calling from a young age to serve others and the nation. I asked my cousin and adopted brother, Peter, for his opinion. He told me, "No way!" and laughed so hard that I still remember it to this day. I allowed that to sway my decision away from the military. Have you experienced something similar? Invited and uninvited feedback can hit at any time and affect people of any age. Be mindful of the source, intention, authenticity, and orientation of the feedback. Evaluate if it is objectively and substantively designed and aligned to serve you, your unique gifts, and greater goals.

Information Forward

When you're in a work environment where you get perception- and manipulation-driven information, it's tough to rise to the occasion and be your best self, much less thrive. It can feel like one step forward, two steps back. It's depleting. You may not be able to change the sources of data and feedback, but you can learn to recognize those environments early so you can decide if and how you want to operate and protect yourself, and ultimately, if it's the right environment for you long-term. You may decide you need to find an atmosphere where you can be received and treated in a data-driven way.

Recognize what sources of information and types of feedback can fortify and help you perform at your best. Then, set out to create those information networks, intersections, and settings where you can receive the type of substantive information that feels more like tailwinds than headwinds. Most importantly, do not let the perceptions from others stop you from doing what you want and being who you are.

So, reader, now it's your turn to apply what you have learned. Analyze the information you've been given here and ask yourself if it is data-, perception-, or manipulation-based. Back up your answer with proof. What's your informed intuition telling you?

The CodeBreaker Mindset™ Takeaways

- There are three types of information and feedback: data-driven, perception-driven, and manipulation-driven.
- Data-driven information and feedback will enable you to compete better in any aspect of life. When the substance matches the form, there is a high probability that the information is data-driven. Beware of perception-driven and manipulation-driven information.
- Information and feedback intended and designed to help you advance, even if it is a tough message, will feel more like a tailwind than a headwind. Information and pointers that feel like a headwind may be an attack, serving the other person, or an agenda that is not in your best interest.
- Vet, triangulate, and octogonulate those sources of input to know what is a verifiable, independent fact versus distortion.
- Base your professional judgments and decisions on substance, not form.

Chapter 9

The Status Quo Is Not Your Friend

> It is not the critic who counts; not the man who points out how the strong man stumbles or where the doer of deeds could have done better. The credit belongs to the man who is actually in the arena, whose face is marred by dust and sweat and blood; who strives valiantly; who errs, and comes up short again and again, because there is no effort without error or shortcoming; but who knows the great enthusiasms, the great devotions; who spends himself in a worthy cause; who at the best knows in the end the triumph of high achievement, and who at the worst, if he fails, at least he fails while daring greatly, so that his place shall never be with those cold and timid souls who knew neither victory nor defeat.[33]
>
> —Theodore Roosevelt, twenty-sixth
> President of the United States

Each one of us was born to actively participate in life—we were born to create, not live under artificial ceilings. Sometimes that creativity bumps up against someone else's status quo. New thoughts and ways of doing things can mess with the person who wants things to stay the same. This can make the creative thinker reluctant to speak up and share ideas, especially if they are naturally conflict-avoidant. But there's a cost to remaining quiet.

We start dreaming and reaching below our potential.

Our life purpose gets diminished.

We miss out on the benefits of personal and professional growth.

Our unique light gets dimmed.

CodeBreakers know when to go with the flow and when to raise their hand and ask the question that'll help people consider new ideas.

This chapter will encourage you not to allow other people's thinking to put limitations on your life. Their thinking is not always the best, especially given the agents of chaos. Many of us like the structure and support that come from conforming. Unfortunately, structure and support also limit us. In today's world, especially, the dynamic, rapid pace of change being whirled at us makes conformity no longer viable or safe. In this environment, toeing the line is a negative. It's actually dangerous to our careers and well-being because bolder thinking and action are required. If you want to be relevant, compete, and succeed, you're better off not conforming. Status quo thinking is not your friend. At best, it's a zero-sum game. At worst, it leaves you in a deficit.

The CodeBreaker Mindset™ Equation and Status Quo

The CodeBreaker Mindset™ is a blueprint for those who want to break free from the constraints and artificial ceilings of traditional ways of thinking. The CodeBreaker Mindset™ Equation can help you break through the tangible and intangible barriers. The status quo contradicts The CodeBreaker

Mindset™ Equation and causes a significant headwind. It would have you believe everything is as it appears to be and skim through life without thinking for yourself.

Being Shot Down

Have you ever had an idea that would improve your employer's work-flow, save money or time, or make processes more efficient? You decide to approach your manager with the idea, and it gets shot down or dismissed. This could be for a number of reasons. Maybe it wasn't such a good idea, or the boss doesn't have the bandwidth to consider anything that doesn't solve an immediate problem. Perhaps your boss worries your shiny new idea will overshadow their efforts with the higher-ups. So you're told, "This is the way it is," or "This is the way we've always done it—we're not changing."

To an employee who is creative and intelligent, few things could be more dispiriting to hear. The manager has just slammed the door in the face of ingenuity. A statement like, "This is how we've always done it," conditions a person to fall in line, to rise only to the minimum expectation.

The manager, intentionally or not, has motivated the employee to be a follower. In other words, do what you're told and don't ask questions. It serves the masses to keep people in line, in check, and constrained to a box. Many companies and bosses say they want their employees to be leaders. However, are the environment and values predisposed to nurturing leadership qualities, independent thinking, creativity, and innovation?

In many cases, especially at larger organizations, it is more difficult for real innovation to be born and blossom at scale. The multiple layers of people, processes, and systems, married with corresponding insecurity, scarcity mindset, and politics, are the biggest barriers to innovation. This is true for individuals, teams, and units. Thus, the default behavior becomes status quo because, more times than not, that behavior is not penalized, and may even be implicitly celebrated.

The status quo, in many contexts, translates to mediocrity or being average at best. This is similar to our discussion around the cons of normal distribution in chapter 3.

Be an Independent Thinker and Chart Your Own Path

In my career, I pierced barriers and shattered ceilings across more than six varying global industries by harnessing elements of The CodeBreaker Mindset™ Equation—knowing the rules of the game, learning to pivot when needed, and being watchful for serendipity. I didn't always wait to be invited into conversations. In some instances, if I had waited, I would still be waiting! I tried to avoid group- or crowd-think and come up with out-of-the-box ideas to add value to the stakeholders I was serving.

I could have stayed in banking and had a fruitful career over the long term. But I felt a pull to attend HBS and expand my horizons. I didn't know what that choice would do for my future—it was a nonlinear move. By the way, something that may seem linear today may be nonlinear in the future. This is an important point. You don't know how your life is going to play out. Studying the school's motto, "leaders who make a difference," on the beautiful cherry-blossom-lined campus in Cambridge, Massachusetts, awakened my passion to be of service to the world through journalism, thought leadership, and sharing information.

It's easy to follow what everyone else is doing. Groupthink has a gravitational pull that seems to shut off your own thoughts and hypnotizes you to flow with the masses. Yes, there are efficiencies to be gained by understanding what the masses are doing, but that may not be what's optimal for you. Value is always created on the margin, on the edge, in uniqueness. The most successful people do not adhere to the masses. Invent your own algorithm or equation for your pursuit path to progress.

Applied Intelligence Quotient, Emotional Quotient, Cultural Quotient, and Holistic Quotient

Of the agents of chaos, technology and AI are democratizing information at high speeds. As more knowledge is available to the world, so grows the propensity for more groupthink. If everyone is participating in similar schools, internships, volunteerism, and job paths, where is the competitive advantage?

With technology and AI, getting ahead will come from deep analytics and applied thinking. This means not fitting into the norms but assembling the ingredients in your own unique way. As technology and AI commoditize knowledge, information, and the intelligence quotient (IQ), leaping forward will come from applied IQ, applied emotional quotient (EQ), applied cultural quotient (CQ), and the aggregation of all quotients into the creation of a new category of holistic quotient (HQ).

Applied IQ is advanced analytics. Not computational analytics, that's not enough. But deep insights to uncover the "so what" in any data and analysis. In analyzing companies, whether financed by private equity, venture capital backed, or publicly traded on stock markets, there is an emphasis on investing in business models generating competitive advantage through the notion of a flywheel. This involves enterprises finding elements and processes that it has figured out how to uniquely link and operate in a way that creates self-fueling momentum and accelerated growth.

Going back to elementary education, many of us were taught when writing stories to ask these essential questions: Who? What? Where? When? Why? How? This is the original framework for finding the flywheel. These six questions are already mainstream; however, we don't usually frame them in the context of a flywheel. The agents of chaos, especially AI, will only make the flywheel concept a requirement in business and life. Being competitive and relevant requires absorbing and integrating this original flywheel into our core being of how we think, communicate, and operate. This then becomes our minimum baseline of knowledge and analysis, or in other words, applied IQ, applied EQ, applied CQ, and applied HQ. The new status quo of thinking and innovating. However, it's the nonlinear multiplicative and exponential sum of these parts that creates the new category of holistic quotient, analogous to quantum computing, as a way we can stay in the driver's seat in the explosive proliferation of technology and AI.

Status Quo When the Bandwidth Is Full

There are times when the best we can do is maintain the status quo. When we're surrounded by pressure, sometimes winning is equivalent to showing up on autopilot. You may not have additional bandwidth or the courage to act independently. Maybe you're dealing with the stresses and strains of life. Or you have too many irons in the fire, health issues, or grief from losing a loved one. Your reserves of intelligence and emotional dexterity may be low. The resilience of your mind and heart may be unable to generate the ideas and fervor to thrust through. It's more than okay to fall in line for as long as you need.

However, while the status quo is not intrinsically bad, be mindful that in many instances it will not be the way you discover your full self and the numerous possibilities within you. After you can carve out the time to rest, replenish, recover, and lift yourself to a new plateau of internal grounding and fortification, propel out of the status quo to the canvas of creation that awaits.

Leaders and High Performers Are Always Inventing

Let's go back to the example of when your boss shot down your idea. Did you go back to your desk and stew over the interaction? Did you think something was wrong with you?

Status quo thinking would say, *Accept what they say. Don't defy the boss; just go along to get along.* But what's lost when you shut your mouth and get back in line? How about your self-worth, enthusiasm to make a difference, and precious energy, to name a few? When you come to work the next day, are you energized to contribute and animated with those around you? No, your flame dimmed. Self-doubt crept in.

Not breaking out of line can keep you stifled in personal growth and evolution. The price can also be steep in terms of opportunity cost or economic loss because you resolved to be on autopilot or have blinders on. Don't relinquish yourself or defer to someone who tells you to accept things the way they are. Are they the oracle? Is anyone? Because when the economy, business, or market forces change, as they inevitably will, you'll be left and forgotten.

With the agents of chaos, there is no foundation, as the foundation is constantly changing. Relying on the status quo will increase your rate of obsolescence and disqualify you from being a contender in the game.

Blackstone

CASE STUDY

Jon Korngold, Blackstone, Global Head of Blackstone Growth

Finance, as an industry, is defined and hierarchical. Whether traditional financial services such as investment banking or alternatives such as hedge funds, private equity, or venture capital, each requires strong technical and analytical skills. A person looks for deals that provide profit, cash flow, and significant valuation gains in the least amount of time.

Many organizations in these areas are large, highly structured, regulated entities. It's easy to be routine and lean on defined playbooks, looking to replicate other people's deals, transactions, trades, and ideas. In this industry, without much effort, you can fall into the trap of status quo thinking, especially given the culture and dynamics of the industry.

But you're not like everyone else. So, how do you come up with your own playbook?

Blackstone's Innovation in Growth Equity

Jon Korngold did just that by reimagining the growth equity business at Blackstone. After a distinguished multi-decade career at platinum-standard financial services firms such as Goldman Sachs and General Atlantic, Jon was recruited to Blackstone, the largest alternative asset manager in the world with a trillion-plus dollars in assets under management. Blackstone owns companies that are trailblazers in their respective industries, such as Spanx, Ancestry, and Bumble. Jon took on the role of Global Head of Blackstone Growth, the growth equity business that he joined the firm to create.

To share some context, growth equity sits at the middle of private equity and venture capital. According to Investopedia, "Private equity firms buy companies and overhaul them to earn a profit when the business is sold again."[34] "Venture capital is financing given to startup companies and small businesses that are seen as having the potential to generate high rates of growth and above-average returns, often fueled by innovation or by carving out a new industry niche."[35]

Instead of following the status quo in growth equity investing, Jon combined the best-in-class practices of private equity that Blackstone was known for with his expertise in late stage growth equity investing. Jon says, "Those growth equity firms that can align themselves with the largest base of strategic and operational infrastructure will have a far better chance of creating more consistent value through economic cycles using operational acumen rather than this index fund of private technology assets that so much of the industry has devolved into. The thesis that resonated with Blackstone is that instead of having a venture heritage approach to growth equity investing, take a private equity approach to portfolio construction. This means having a very concentrated portfolio and a private equity approach to risk management and operational involvement [and] being really hands-on with the companies with whom you partner. How do you cut off a lot of that left tail of risk and volatility often associated with growth and technology investing? If you can do that, you could become the 'sleep well at night' growth equity fund. Growth and venture are the last bastion of a cottage industry in the equity space. If you can weaponize the cottage industry by gaining access to the resources uniquely available to a firm with more than a trillion dollars in assets, you can bring those end-state operating resources to companies in their proverbial adolescence. You can help many of these companies fight way above their weight class and in doing so, minimize some of the execution risks that are associated with going from adolescence to adulthood."

Jon distinguishes that he used a mindset that "wasn't a venture capitalist. I wasn't looking to make one hundred investments and have thirty of them go bust and fifty of them go sideways and twenty of them end up making your fund. Maybe it's my days at Goldman Sachs and the industrial buyout space that made me think about risk from a private equity lens. Blackstone realized there was such a rich vein of opportunity to help these companies with access to a set of resources that historically had never been introduced to the growth equity market. It just felt like the right moment for me to try that blank sheet of paper and see what we might be able to do if it's not encumbered by decades of a certain way of approaching the industry."

Keeping Your Pattern Recognition Fresh

On investing and helping companies withstand economic cycles and headwinds, Jon emphasizes, "There's always this balance of wanting to draw on your pattern recognition, but recognizing that sometimes it can be stale. You have to remind yourself that the world around you is changing so quickly that if you allow yourself to be unfairly and unnecessarily rooted to what you know, you're not going to be in a position to be as agile. You're going to get caught flat-footed.

"There were a lot of times when I went into certain situations in our investment committee dogmatic about knowing this area well. I've gone in saying that I've invested in five companies in this space, and I'm telling you, this is where it's going to go. But sometimes, it takes a fresh set of eyes to push your thinking, because you realize there might be huge subsectors I summarily dismissed because of some unfounded bias, rather than bringing a fresh set of eyes to a problem. It's important to realize that you sometimes need to get out of your own way and that we will most often make the correct decision as a group rather than as an individual."

Jon is a leader who didn't fall prey to status quo thinking. Despite already being at the top of his game, he was and is intentional and conscious about how to innovate. He thought outside of the box and imagined new ways to create value, the results of which have brought significant returns on investment for stakeholders over the years.

Why Do People Stick to the Status Quo?

We've shared some of the consequences of blending into the current state and not questioning things. Why, then, do some cling to the status quo?

Fear

Many of us are afraid that people will laugh at us or we'll be penalized for our ideas. Or we've experienced resistance in the past when we spoke up, perhaps starting in childhood, which caused us to fear putting our ideas out there. Most of us want to feel accepted and understood when we take risks and contribute suggestions. If people beat us down, we don't feel safe expressing ourselves.

Trauma

Many who have tried to be independent thinkers have faced repercussions, sometimes harsh, for not abiding by the laws in place. People are more delicate than ever due to all the agents of chaos. Fragility, vulnerability, pain, disappointment, and unexpected hijackings (see chapter 6) can all give birth to trauma. This may result in debilitating our capability and bandwidth to reject the status quo, or being afraid.

Predisposition or Preconditioning

We have a predisposition to stick to the status quo. Becoming a Code-Breaker requires that we rewire some of our thinking. For example, you get a certain pre-wiring from your family, friends, community, school, religion, volunteerism, extracurricular activities, and jobs. Think about all the conditioning you received, explicit and implicit, from birth to eighteen years old. How much of that programming do you stick with today?

Were you encouraged in your life to stay in your lane—whether in education, career, relationships, or geographically? Or were you nurtured to explore the world, switch it up, and try new things? This preconditioning is ingrained on a cellular level. Being a conscious, independent thinker may come more naturally for some.

During a famous speech in the 1960s, Robert F. Kennedy (former United States Attorney General and brother of President John F. Kennedy) quoted George Bernard Shaw by saying, "Some people see things as they are and say, why? I dream things that never were and say, why not?"[36] If you're the person who runs with the current state of things and asks, "Why change?," now is the opportunity to open your mind to think differently.

New Ideas Not Welcome

If you work in a controlling environment that has a culture of rigidity, there's not much you can do beyond deciding if you want to stay in that ecosystem or leave. If your boss or teammates consistently eject your ideas, then you have to ask yourself, *Am I in an environment where I can thrive?* Sometimes, the issue is not you but what is around you. Just understand the trade-offs you are making by staying there. Trade-offs that may include potentially stifling your creativity, imagination, voice, productivity, and ultimately, self-purpose. Staying can increase your rate of obsolescence and force you to stick with legacy or analog practices, which eventually impairs the growth and staying power of your mind, skillset, and capabilities.

Skimming to Survive

At the end of the first chapter, I shared a quote from a novel titled *Lullaby*. Here's an excerpt worth highlighting.

> [Big Brother]'s making sure your attention is always filled. And this being fed, it's worse than being watched. With the world always filling you, no one has to worry about what's in your mind. With everyone's imagination atrophied, no one will ever be a threat to the world.[37]

Whether we like it or not, we all experience atrophy. We become overwhelmed by and over-subscribed to countless responsibilities in our lives. We have more tech gadgets and platforms leeching for our engagement than we can handle, countless logins and passwords, and spend multiple hours on the phone with help desks for everything—banking, credit cards, healthcare, insurance, education, social security, travel, and so on.

We are bombarded with real and fake data on social media. We can't read and digest everything flashing through our five senses, so we scan. We skim to survive, keep up, and get through it. We skim to feel that we have read everything and aren't missing out. The result is that our holistic beings are atrophying.

Social Media and Skimming to the Status Quo

This is amplified by social media, which gives quick access to information at any time on any subject. Students research and get their data from the short-form videos on TikTok. But we aren't blowing the whistle on the fact that these social media sites are flooded with distorted information.

PBS News reported that "Researchers at New York University have concluded that social media is not an accurate reflection of society, but more like a funhouse mirror distorted by a small but vocal minority of extreme outliers."[38] It is also rife with biases. Even LinkedIn, which is perceived as data-driven, has some bias. These sites might give you data on popular history and culture, or from "popular" content creators or classify someone or something as a "Top Post" by their own algorithm that has nothing to do with fact verification. You may get a slice of "understanding," but your education on the topic is drastically insufficient.

All of that contributes to atrophy. How do we cope?

We skim through life.

We skim when we're thinking, reading, writing, feeling, speaking, acting, processing, or operating anything. On social media, we speed read, scan, and scroll. Social media is one of the biggest reasons for our skimming mindset and behavior. The core functionality of social media and the mobile device is to scroll and swipe for information. Many become addicted looking for instant satiation. The senses are being soothed by getting information on anything and everything we want in ten seconds or less, but still, we scream that it takes too long.

Our scanning behavior impacts our ability to concentrate or pay attention. We may not be fully present in a conversation or interaction because subconsciously, we've trained our minds to jump around, needing the distraction that is inherently present in social media, where scrolling swirls new images across the screen every second.

The result of skimming is a high propensity to stick to the status quo, because anything else takes up too much time, energy, and effort. We're not giving ourselves the time to explicitly read and explore, and then to think and process. This also creates a dynamic where we sleepwalk through life, side swipe, and show up lazier.

In the fast culture we are in, we are looking for instant gratification. This is especially true given that we have the largest intergenerational workforce. Each generation of talent has different frames of contextual understanding and reference, work ethic, behavioral norms, values, and standards.

The default setting and incentive structure are to bask in the status quo.

Erosion of the Baseline

The agents of chaos, whether technology, AI, mental health crisis, corrosion of community, or misinformation, have dismantled what's defined as baseline in so many vectors of life, especially as it relates to minimum levels of knowledge, work ethic, and performance at work. This means people, processes, and systems that hug the status quo will, over time, become less competitive, and antiquated. The result is an erosion of general knowledge about what's required to stand out in professional realms.

Sleepwalking

According to a LinkedIn study, about a third of professionals in the United States are "career sleepwalking." The study reports, "Nearly half of all professionals ages thirty-five to forty-four aren't sure what their career path should look like, even after spending more than a decade in the workforce." Some feel "they are on a treadmill going nowhere." However, "80% of those under 24 would consider switching careers (function or industry)."[39]

Workers who are sleepwalking may show a lack of consciousness and urgency to deliver the most optimal output for themselves and the company. In environments where employees are disengaged, that modality becomes ingrained into firm culture. If employees are mostly watching the clock until they can leave, they fall into a rut. Autopilot does not bring forward fresh ideas, optimal productivity, or ensure that the execution of the work is performed with low risk and low error rates. At a basic level, the person may start to give up on themselves and the positive possibilities for their life.

Slumbering through the day results in a high probability that you will cling to those and what you know. For example, if you attend a conference and only talk to the people with whom you're already familiar, you're giving and getting the bare minimum. To maximize the ROI, return on the intersection (see chapter 11, "Creating Ecosystems and Network Effects"), be awake and alert to engage the new faces you meet. If everyone in your clique is attending the same breakout session at the event, why not check out a different session? Separate from the pack and position yourself to meet and learn about new people and things.

The more homogenous you keep yourself and your ecosystem, the less access you have to new ideas, creativity, and innovation. This atrophies your mindset and your mental and emotional muscles.

Risk Aversion and Anxiety

There is some level of risk aversion and anxiety in every human. Most of us don't like change and ambiguity. We take comfort in certainty and the path of least resistance to achieving anything. On top of that, the more our bandwidth is stretched and over-subscribed, the less elasticity we have to take calculated gambles and absorb unpredictable outcomes or variability from expectations.

Research from PR Newswire shows that adults in the United States like to play it safe. "65% prefer the consistency and stability of staying with one employer rather than taking the risk of moving around; 35% prefer to take the risk of making changes (e.g., employer, field, starting a business, etc.) because they believe it has a higher potential for success/happiness than inaction." In relationships, "66% stick close to the friends they already have, not necessarily because they're uninterested in forming new relationships, but rather because they tend to avoid taking chances socially; 34% put themselves out there and take chances socially because they love the prospect of forming new friendships/relationships."[40]

Risk aversion is not static. An appetite for risk can evolve at any time and is contingent on a plethora of factors such as age and stage of life, experiences, specific scenarios, risk versus reward profile, motivations, incentives, etc. InsideBE writes that "An individual's desire to avoid risk can be gauged by what they're willing to forgo to avoid any risk whatsoever. The extent of their 'sacrifice' is known as the risk premium. If the payoff of a decision equals or exceeds a person's risk premium, the person will become indifferent to the risk and choose the uncertain option."[41]

Another cognitive factor at play is that "People tend to vastly overestimate the small probabilities, thereby exaggerating their perception of risk in the given situation."[42] So, what to do? Be mindful of this. Examine the situation and understand the true nature, scope, and extent of the risk. Is your assessment of risk data-, perception-, or manipulation-driven? (Refer back to chapter 8 to review the definitions.) It's for you to determine how much of your risk appetite you want to open up over time, and what steps you can take to build your muscle in this regard.

Sometimes we are our own worst enemy, or the perception- and manipulation-based people around us hype us into thinking there is more risk than there is. Many things are not that deep. Researchers at InsideBE also say, "Don't forget to look at the bigger picture! When viewed in a vacuum, every decision can seem too risky, but when imagined over your entire lifespan, they'll end up seeming rather minuscule."[43]

In a workplace and team context, the same research says, "Managers should be evaluated based on a portfolio of outcomes and not the success or failure of a single project. By taking a more understanding stance in dealing with failure, you can depersonalize it. This breeds managers who are more comfortable with handling risk without fearing the detrimental consequences to their career."[44]

Forbes revealed that employers who encourage employees to take risks may benefit from less frequent turnover because "Every new project, role, or job creates an opportunity to learn. Build a culture where employees welcome risks by enabling them to make mistakes without harsh career consequences. The goal is to build a culture that encourages staff to try new things and dabble in new functional areas."[45]

Not Conforming in Academia

CASE STUDY

Dr. David Thomas, Morehouse College, President

Dr. David Thomas is no stranger to risk and independent thinking. He's the twelfth president of Morehouse College, a top-ranked historically black college and university (HBCU), and the only historically black private liberal arts college for men in the United States. Dr. Thomas has brought in more than $240 million in fundraising for the school. No stranger to the highest levels of academia, before Morehouse, he served as the H. Naylor Fitzhugh Professor of Business Administration at Harvard Business School, as the dean and William R. Berkley Chair at Georgetown University's McDonough School of Business, and as an assistant professor at the Wharton School of Business at the University of Pennsylvania. Dr. Thomas led the redesign of the MBA curriculum at McDonough and a successful $130 million capital campaign. He's an award-winning author and internationally recognized as a scholar and contemporary thought leader in areas such as organizational behavior, management, and executive development.

Diversity

In academia, there are perceived safer and less risk-averse areas in which to specialize. Dr. Thomas was ahead of the curve in his areas of concentration. "Timing is important in my field," he says. "I was studying issues of diversity going back to the 1980s. Ronald Reagan was President. We were writing articles about how affirmative action was dead. That morphed into this topic called 'diversity.' There was a study in the late eighties called Workforce 2000 about the browning of the American workforce. CEOs were asking the dean at Harvard if he knew about this topic and workforce diversity. He went back to some senior faculty and said, 'What do we know about this?' They said, 'We don't know anything.' He said, 'Well, who's doing work on it out there in the world?' That led them to me.

"I was at the Wharton School then, one of five people in the country doing work on that topic. The world caught up with me. I didn't catch up with the world.

"So my timing was good because I followed my instincts. And the other thing that's part of the game in academia for black people is you can't be marginalized, especially if you're at a business school. So I made a point of mastering all the tools, and the things people value beyond just whether or not you were being published."

He went beyond the status quo.

Georgetown University's McDonough School of Business

When Professor Thomas became the dean of Georgetown University's McDonough School of Business, he had to architect how he was going to infuse change into a school that had built a strong brand and reputation for fifty-four years. "Number one is if you're going to change an institution that's been relatively successful, you need to set your change agenda very early and move very fast," he says. "Coming in and saying, 'I'm going to spend a year to learn the place,' that's a year that the forces against change will harden and become more difficult for you to move.

"I picked five themes and said, 'These are the five themes we're going to organize around for the next five years.' And picked two or three projects that people said were impossible to do, and we did them to great success. We transformed that place. Same thing here at Morehouse."

Morehouse College

"Number two, discover the talent that is hidden in your organization," he explains. "One of my great blessings at Morehouse is that there are two people who today, in my view, are more critical than I am to the college continuing to thrive. When I got here, they were buried. But I paid attention to them and noticed that everything I asked them to do, they achieved above and beyond my expectations. They became critical players for me and were part of why we were able to make a huge difference."

How did he identify key talent who weren't conformists and would think outside of the box? "It's all about listening as a leader. I would listen for who was listening to me. Oftentimes, what listening for me means is you're willing to put the interests of the school ahead of your own. We have to break down the silos. So I look for the people who do this by being willing to give up something that might be more beneficial to them.

"Change the structure of the organization to reflect your strategic intent is another lesson. At Georgetown, we had four different MBA products, and we brought them together under one organizational entity. That was critical and highly resisted."

Billionaire Donors

There are many brilliantly similar academic institutions and HBCUs. When it comes to attracting billionaire donors, like Vista Equity's Chairman and CEO Robert Smith, Netflix's founder Reed Hastings, philanthropist MacKenzie Scott, and media icon Oprah Winfrey, how did Morehouse fly ahead?

Dr. Thomas says, "What I try to tell my team is, every little thing we do tells people who we are. So we've got to exceed their expectations. The biggest thing my team did that really transformed how our board saw us was that they watched the weather reports. One time, it was going to rain, and they had umbrellas for everybody, and they had ordered cars to take people back to their hotels. Well, I'm also on the board of two or three publicly traded companies, Fortune 500 companies, and the largest asset manager in the world, Vanguard. That's the kind of thing you would expect from those companies. You don't expect that from a small, relatively under-resourced college like Morehouse."

Career Advice

Graduates seek guidance from Dr. Thomas because they aren't getting career opportunities in their organization. They wanted to know if it had anything to do with race. He would ask the students, "Is it a good company?" And they would say, "Yeah, it's a good company. Other than my disappointment, I like working there." Dr. Thomas says, "That's the way I felt about Harvard Business School. It was the best place I ever worked. I was the happiest I'd ever been there. But what I would say to people is, 'Well, maybe you should go out and see if there's any place else in the world that can see you the way you see yourself.' I saw myself as having the qualities to be a dean." When Dr. Thomas applied for and was not selected as the tenth dean of HBS, he subsequently pursued and became the twelfth dean of the McDonough School of Business at Georgetown.

Practice Not Conforming to the Status Quo

A recurring theme from the leaders we have heard from is the importance of embracing your uniqueness, whether it's your own style of thinking, creating, or acting. Here's some encouragement on how to build the muscle of not conforming to the status quo.

Practice Flexing Your Independence Muscle

Not conforming is hard. Over time, it becomes easier with practice. Every time you make a decision that is right for you, not based on conforming to anyone else's standards, it is like exercising a weak muscle. You don't have to turn your world upside down or make a big impact all at once. Start practicing the flex with something small. Choose a few simple goals to start with.

Practice the Art of Making Your Own Rules

Without the norms and rules of conformity handcuffing your journey, CodeBreakers are free to make their own playbook, based on what they think is best for their life. Here are some guideposts:

- Continually ask yourself, *What makes sense for me? What do I want to pursue?* Checking in with yourself in this way keeps you on track.
- Choose your battles. Don't overload your plate with too many difficult goals at once. Pace yourself and be selective about what you pursue.
- Set boundaries. Don't be too extreme. CodeBreakers make their own rules, but they still live by a code of conduct based on kindness, empathy, and respect for others.

You Are a Unique Being. Wholeheartedly Embrace Your Uniqueness.

We are all unique individuals, but we often ignore or downplay that which sets us apart. Strong forces in society try to pressure us into turning away from our originality so we will look and behave exactly like everyone else. We might even be afraid that we will be penalized for being unique. In many legacy paradigms, being different or unusual is not thought of as a strength. There is incredible power in being the one and only you, so embrace it. This is a mindset shift for many. Embracing all of you means no longer hiding parts of your identity or tempering your thoughts and opinions to make others feel comfortable.

Feeling Disoriented Is Normal

You're not making a mistake. When you veer outside of the lines of conformity, it may feel strange and disorienting. You've lived inside one set of circumstances for so long that after breaking free, you might believe you've made a mistake. This is normal. It will take time to find your bearings, but you will. The more you experience not conforming, the easier it will become.

Develop Your Spine of Steel

People might not understand why you are suddenly embracing a different path, and you might face some backlash, judgment, or criticism. When you become different, or not the follower of what everyone else is doing, don't be surprised if people try to beat you back in line or pull you down so you won't grow and change.

When you take an opposite stand on an issue, there may also be polarization. It may make you an outsider. They may turn away from you or lash out. Others may interpret your independent behavior as strength, confidence, or boldness. Many don't like that and are afraid of it because it's not something they understand or can relate to. It's not something they have the spine of steel to do, and it makes them feel inadequate. Be prepared to be uncomfortable. That feeling won't last forever.

The CodeBreaker Mindset™ Takeaways

- Don't be limited or controlled by someone else's status quo.
- Everything that's been created by humans that is status quo today was a change and an innovation at one point in time. New developments are only new until the next wave of incremental or nonlinear change.
- Change is the new status quo. Embrace it.

Chapter 10

Become What You Believe

Audentes fortuna iuvat.[46]
(Fortune favors the bold.)

—Virgil, ancient Roman poet

You are going to encounter a situation where you really want something. That thing you want will require certain knowledge, skills, relationships, access, resources, and some ingredients that you don't have. You may be viewed as not being the "perfect fit" in someone else's eyes.

Let's talk about this. Is there really such a thing as a perfect candidate for any role or opportunity? Does anyone have the precise education, background, connections, and experience for the things they want to accomplish? Whether you are pursuing your first job, a promotion in the same industry, or a career change, it's highly unlikely that there is a perfect candidate. In this chapter, we're going to focus on how to problem solve any bona fide or perceived gaps in your qualifications.

FOBD—Fear of Being Deficient

Many of us, regardless of how educated, qualified, or experienced we are, may have the feeling of being deficient, or in some way falling short, of the requisites needed to clinch that next job or opportunity. A compound effect to that is when others make us feel in a deficit position—whether data-driven, perception-driven, or manipulation-driven (see chapter 8, "Information Is Power").

You have a choice to make. Do you stay where you are, keep it status quo, and hope the dream opportunity will come knocking on your door? Are you tempted to start making excuses and creating barriers because of the FOBD imposed on you by yourself and/or others? This may instill some self-doubt about what is possible for you to achieve.

Mother Teresa, the Catholic nun and Nobel Peace Prize recipient, championed the underserved through the Missionaries of Charity, a global religious order that helps the poorest populations. This poem was found written on her wall after her death:

Do It Anyway

People are often unreasonable, illogical, and self-centered.
Forgive them anyway.
If you are kind, people may accuse you of selfish, ulterior
motives.
Be kind anyway.
If you are successful, you will win some unfaithful friends
and some genuine enemies.
Succeed anyway.
If you are honest and sincere people may deceive you.
Be honest and sincere anyway.
What you spend years creating, others could destroy overnight.

Create anyway.
If you find serenity and happiness, some may be jealous.
Be happy anyway.
The good you do today, will often be forgotten.
Do good anyway.
Give the best you have, and it will never be enough.
Give your best anyway.
In the final analysis, it is between you and God.
It was never between you and them anyway.[47]

Feel the encouragement from these words. Don't let what you believe or perceive as missing from your qualifications be the reason you don't pursue your goals. Ignore the rules and barriers created by your self-doubt, gatekeepers, or those trying to hold you back. It's crucial to uncover what the necessary ingredients are for any pursuit. This is where knowing the unwritten rules is incredibly important. There are always work-arounds to help you reach a goal. You just have to find them.

Hollywood: Fake It till You Make It

To bring this to life, we will look at two examples from Hollywood, widely considered the media and entertainment center of the world. Scaling the walls of this fortress to gain entrance is incredibly difficult, whether you're behind the scenes, like Oscar-winning producer Bruce Cohen, or vying for a role in front of the camera, like Tony Award–winning actor BD Wong.

What is the perfect constitution of a Hollywood A-lister? There isn't one. Anyone trying to break into Hollywood, much less someone who possesses the staying power to remain at the top of the game, will be missing ingredients. Yet that does not stop those who are driven by passion and intention.

Dress Up What You Do Have

CASE STUDY

Bruce Cohen, Academy and Tony Award–winning and Emmy-Nominated Producer

Bruce Cohen has had a spectacular and enduring forty-plus-year career in Hollywood, winning the Academy Award for Best Picture for *American Beauty*, as well as additional Best Picture nominations for *Milk* and *Silver Linings Playbook*. He's also won the Tony for Best Play for *The Inheritance*. He's highly sought-after in the A-list circles, including having worked with famed actors Bradley Cooper, Robert DeNiro, Colman Domingo, James Franco, Jennifer Lawrence, Sean Penn, and Oprah Winfrey. But Bruce's career path wasn't always lined in gold.

When Bruce first moved to Los Angeles, he began as an intern for Warner Bros. Here's how Bruce describes going from not having the right ingredients to launching his film career as a Directors Guild of America (DGA) trainee on legendary director Steven Spielberg's *The Color Purple*.

Hill Street Blues

"My first DGA training job at Warner Bros. was on a television series called *Hill Street Blues*, which was a very successful, prestigious television show. I was on the show's fifth season, and by that point, it had redefined television and was winning Emmys. It was a critical hit, a commercial hit. The mindset on the set of *Hill Street Blues* was every single person on that cast and crew showed up every morning to make extraordinary, superlative, groundbreaking television. Not just good, not just great, but something very special that the audience had never seen before.

"After about three months on the show, even though the season was still going, the Warner Bros. training program took me off the show because they wanted trainees to get lots of different experience. Suddenly, I'm out of work. On my last day of *Hill Street Blues*, a couple of different people said to me, 'You're the best trainee we've ever had.' That was very meaningful to me because it was my first job, and I was something like the fifteenth trainee they'd had over the five seasons. I thought, *Okay, that's good. Maybe I'm onto something.*

"Three months went by, and I have no work. I'm not getting paid. I'm ready, waiting for my next gig. I actually had to file for unemployment, which was really hard. Then finally, one morning, I called Dina Bachelor at the training program; she was terrific, and I said, 'Dina, I've been out of work for three months. I'm collecting unemployment. I had the most incredible time on *Hill Street Blues*. When am I going to have another job in this training program?'"

Steven Spielberg

"She said, 'Well, there's this movie and they're interviewing three candidates. Most movies we don't have trainees interview; we just assign them, but this movie is a really big deal. So we agreed to let them meet three choices. They only wanted to meet people who had been in the program for two or more years, were super experienced, and had done a great job. But the interviews are this afternoon, and I've only filled two of the slots. And since you did such a great job on *Hill Street Blues*, and since you happened to call me this morning, I'll let you take the third slot and go interview for this movie at Warner Bros. called *Moonsong*.'"

Bruce continues, "Warner Bros. is where I had just been clerking. So I called my friend Judith who worked there. She was the assistant to the president of Warner Bros. I said, 'I have an interview for this movie called *Moonsong*.' She said, 'My God, that's the secret code name for *The Color Purple* directed by Steven Spielberg.'

"This is the post-*E.T.*, post-*Raiders of the Lost Ark*, post-*Jaws* Steven Spielberg. So I knew I'd had a huge stroke of luck. Now I have to convert it into a job. This could change my life, so I thought, *What are the tools at my disposal to get this job?*

"I knew my disadvantages. My goal going into the interview was to try and make sure that the second assistant director and the first assistant director would call someone at *Hill Street Blues* to check my references. At some point in the interview, I mentioned that they call and check my references, and I remember thinking at the time, *They're not going to do that.* The interview went well, but as I'm leaving, I thought, *Have I achieved my goal of trying to blow past the disadvantages I have to actually get this job? No, I haven't.*

"When the interview ended, as I'm leaving, I stop at the door—sort of dramatically because suddenly I'm thinking all this in my head and the interview's over, I'm out the door—and turn back around. They ask me, 'What?'

"'I just have one more thing to say. For you, I'm just another candidate that you're interviewing. But for me, this opportunity could change the entire course of my life and career. I have one small ask before I leave.'

"'What is it?'"

"'Would you just promise me before I go out the door that you will call someone at *Hill Street Blues*? It's just thirty seconds of your life, but it could change my entire life.'

"They looked into my eyes and said, 'Yes, we will call.'

"I ended up getting the job. Within the three or four first days of work, I asked them, 'I'm curious, why did you hire me?' They said, 'Well, we weren't going to, even though we loved you in the interview, but you didn't really have the experience. But then, you seemed so insistent about us calling *Hill Street Blues* that we felt like we had to do it. It was late when we remembered, so we picked up the phone at 9 PM and didn't really feel anyone would still be there. Scott Brazil [one of the highly reputable executive producers of the Emmy Award–winning show] answered the phone. The staff and the assistants were gone, or he would never have picked up the phone. He was clearly very hurried and didn't really want to be talking to whoever it was. The AD [Assistant Director] said, "So sorry to bother you, Mr. Brazil, but we just wanted to check a reference on this trainee Bruce Cohen, who we're interviewing." Scott Brazil yelled, "If you don't hire that kid, it's the biggest mistake you'll ever make," and hung up the phone.'

"They hired me and I ended up working with Steven Spielberg and his producers at the time, Kathy Kennedy and Frank Marshall, for the rest of my career. Kathy and Frank are the reason why I'm a producer because I saw them producing on *The Color Purple* and on the next five or six movies that I assistant directed at Amblin Entertainment, which is Spielberg's production company. When the *American Beauty* script came in to Dan Jinx and me, we took it to Steven Spielberg and he made it at DreamWorks. So literally, that moment, as I had thought it might be, changed my entire life, and set up everything that happened since then."

It's easy to quit. There were different twists and turns when Bruce had the easier option to abort mission. But Bruce had the maniacal desire, drive, and passion to figure it out at all costs. He also showed us what can happen when we dress up and reorient what we have. In addition to raw talent, Bruce was a high performer, such that a respected, award-winning executive in the industry vouched for him, which covered any qualifications he lacked.

Serendipity

Referring to chapter 7, "Serendipity and Informed Intuition," note the number of junctures where serendipity, whether it was preparation, timing, opportunity, energy, or informed intuition, had a role in manifesting Bruce's goal.

If you want an opportunity to play in the game but you're not qualified according to the prospective employer's terms, the following are some suggestions to minimize what you lack and amplify the skills that set you apart from your competition. Some people call this *getting* your foot in the door, but I've always preferred to think of it as *putting* your foot in the door. Because, as we read in Bruce's story, it may mean you take a chance, make a bold assertion, and plead so your position gets heard.

Put Your Foot in the Door

First, Be Highly Competent. It's Just the Price of Admission.

Always be reading, studying, learning, and working to improve. As we talked about in chapter 5, always be prepared. Be willing to do what others won't, get into the details, and learn what is required.

Get Experience Where You Can and Build on It

No one starts at the top. The path to get there isn't always clear. Any role you hunt can be broken down into the following requirement areas:

- Knowledge base (e.g., industry domain, your own relevant intellectual property)
- Hard skills (i.e., technical) and soft skills (i.e., interpersonal)
- Relationships (i.e., Do you need to bring in relationships with clients, vendors, or other stakeholders?)
- Resources (i.e., Can the company and role benefit from any resources or assets that you possess that can be additive, such as funding sources?)
- Access (i.e., Can you provide access to unique assets that create differentiation and advantage, such as critical knowledge, skills, relationships, resources, etc.?)

When you dissect the role requirements into these areas, write down and rank which of these you possess. Then prepare your verbal elevator pitch, or written pitch via your resume, biography, LinkedIn profile, cover letter, etc., that positions and amplifies your strengths. Find ways to leverage the ingredients that you do have and create the appropriate narratives to bridge any gaps. Especially when you don't have all the prescribed ingredients, you need to convince people that the ones you do have are better.

Focus on What You Have, Not on What You Don't

In chapter 2, I touched on some of my journey from investment banking to TV journalism. It's pertinent for me to mention here how I put my foot in the door and made that nonlinear career jump.

I wanted to get into the competitive field of broadcast journalism, but there was one big problem. I did not have the traditional background. I had not studied journalism, nor worked in a local news market, cutting my teeth producing, shooting, and reporting on stories from the field in an agile and scrappy way. I had not gone to school to learn the technical skills of shooting and editing stories. I researched going back to school and getting a journalism degree. The professors and deans at the journalism schools encouraged me to hit the streets, not the classroom, and start reporting.

Domain and Relationships Matter

I was fortunate in that I encountered experienced and former journalists who were willing to teach me the mechanics of the news reporting business. Some were willing to teach me on their own, and some I had to encourage to share their wisdom. They agreed to help because they recognized that I had solid, bona fide business education and industry credentials that would help position me as a credible business news reporter.

What did I dial up and leverage? My knowledge, skills, relationships, and perspective—all valued assets in journalism. I had a business education from reputable schools (Rotman School of Management and HBS), a CPA designation, and years jockeying the highs and lows of Wall Street. I had a wealth of the underlying domain and access to environments that I was embarking to report on. I was able to effectively take the focus off my lack of journalism experience and get them interested in me as a subject matter expert who they said was an effective communicator.

My finance, investment banking, and operator background set me up nicely for being a business reporter and anchor. I had prior experience interacting with and serving all kinds of executives and companies in the Fortune 1000. I was fortunate to have a deep and holistic 360-degree proficiency in how these companies worked. This included understanding the people, processes, systems, different organizational functions, and expertise with macroeconomic and microeconomic factors, company earnings reports, accounting, strategy, marketing, and decision-making at the Fortune 1000 level.

These were the same entities and stories that dominated business news. I had an advanced level of proficiency and market perspective that enabled me to add value to news reporting. My experience gave me an innate understanding of the business leaders I was interviewing as well as the viewers and readers, so crafting smart questions and conducting insightful interviews came naturally to me. However, I still worked continuously to improve and perfect it.

Tell Anyone Who Will Listen What You Are Trying to Do

Networking is a critical component of succeeding professionally, and when you're starting out or looking to jump careers, it's the connections you make that can help you swim to a smarter and smoother transition.

I started to put the word out to anyone who would listen. I would tell friends, strangers, even my seatmates on airplanes, whoever would listen, "Hey, I'm trying to break into journalism. How do I figure this out?"

When I was working on transitioning into journalism, I was serendipitously asked to moderate a panel on economic empowerment with leaders from Philadelphia. There was a PR firm involved in organizing the conference, and I met the CEO. I told her I wanted to break into journalism, and she said, "I have a person working in my company who is a former TV producer, and we'll help you put a reel together." Even though I was new to learning about reels and the lingo, I knew I was creating and following the path to my dreams, despite missing ingredients!

Recognize Opportunity and Take It

Learn to spot openings in the moment and quickly act on them because that's where opportunity lives. When I attended the NABJ Conference, I heard a powerful speech given by Arianna Huffington. She described her journey to securing a publishing deal for one of her early books after receiving roughly thirty-plus rejections. She spoke about the strangers in the forest who come forward to help us on our journeys. Afterward, I introduced myself to Arianna to tell her how much I enjoyed what she had shared. She was on her way out and asked if I wanted to walk and talk.

It was early days for *The Huffington Post* (now *HuffPost*), and she was looking for a diverse group of writers. She felt energy alignment with me and asked, "Would you like to write for *The Huffington Post*?" I told her yes and gave her my information. Boom, thank you, Arianna and serendipity! This provided the path for me to start writing and building my skills and portfolio, as an important skill I needed to develop was journalism writing.

Be Willing to Put Yourself Out There, Even When It's Uncomfortable

Look, it takes nerve to walk up to a person, even more so if the person is famous. That feeling may not go away. You don't know if they're going to be rude and blow you off or take the time to hear you out. You won't know until you gather the courage to do it. But if the occasion presents itself, try to build the muscle to always take the shot. What's the absolute worst thing that could happen? They don't have time to talk or ignore you. Okay, so what? Move on. But the chances are high that by stepping out, you get to meet someone and make a relevant connection, moving you one step closer to your dreams.

Own Who You Are and Start Building a Brand Around It

Be yourself. Everyone else is taken. There is great power in authenticity. The collective impact of all your experiences is powerful. Start building your story around that while finding angles that foster genuine connection with whoever you are trying to convince to give you a chance. People like to hear about unconventional paths and, ultimately, they respect and appreciate those who figure out nontraditional routes. Leverage what makes you different and memorable.

Don't Take On Anyone Else's FOBD

Don't let anyone hammer at you or focus on what you don't have. Remember what we talked about in chapter 8—not everyone is your friend. Understand if the source of the information is data-, perception-, or manipulation-driven. There is more than one way to achieve a goal. Don't let anyone tell you that you have to do this or have to have that. Do your homework and look at the journeys of those you aspire to be. I bet none of them did it the same way or with one set of education, skills, and pedigree.

Most people are missing ingredients. They might have improvised or been able to acquire what was necessary to close the gaps. In some cases, improvisation was enough, or they had a serendipitous relationship that opened the gate. Maybe they were different and won over stakeholders with whatever strengths they did have. However they did it, they didn't let what was missing stop them.

Don't Discount the Hustle Factor

There is great power in showing up, but that's just the beginning. When you attend conferences, dinner parties, retreats, or any kind of event, you can't just go and hope for the best. If you've read this far in the book, you've heard me say this a number of different ways. Life rewards preparation and action. Don't just sit in the back and wait for something to happen. Get up, introduce yourself to people, and be prepared to make the ask.

Have So Much Experience That Nothing Throws You Off

CASE STUDY

BD Wong, Tony Award–winning and Emmy-Nominated Actor

BD Wong has been bold in his journey to manifest something from nothing. BD is known for winning several awards for his performance in *M. Butterfly*, including the Tony Award and Drama Desk Award. Over his illustrious forty-year-plus career in Hollywood and Broadway, he has played roles in hit series such as *Law & Order SVU* and the *Jurassic Park* franchise, as well as Disney's animated film *Mulan*. I explored with BD the behavior patterns and auditioning process for young, relatively inexperienced actors to identify any parallels with The CodeBreaker Mindset™.

BD shares the disappointing experience he had in college: "I was spoiled by my high school teacher, who gave me a lot of confidence and encouragement—I use my relationship with her as a kind of template for what a mentor-mentee relationship can really be—but in college, I was ignored and dismissed. I had enough self-esteem to realize that something was wrong with that, so I dropped out and came to New York to get a street education on how to make a living as a New York actor. I don't recommend dropping out of school, but for me, it worked out well."

Learn the Art of Auditioning

"I broke into the business by auditioning, as one does, but more specifically, by learning the art of auditioning and by being relentless about it," he recalls.

"I went to every single audition that I heard about. I got comfortable auditioning. I'd say a huge key to young actors being successful is their ability to put themselves in front of other people and sell themselves. There are a lot of great actors who are paralyzed by the audition process.

"I had a lot of friends who graduated from college and then had to learn all this stuff that I learned in New York City because they don't really teach it in school. They teach a little bit more now about audition technique, but the real meat of it is doing it.

"I'm such an advocate for college programs really teaching this aspect of auditioning beyond just how to walk into a room. If you were to call it a class, the curriculum would be about preparing yourself, preparation when there's nobody else around, and then the actual experience of walking into a room with strangers. Have so much experience that nothing really throws you off. Auditioning is not really something you can learn except by doing it. I figured out a lot on my own. Anything you do on your own, though, isn't really 'on your own.' There are people around all the time that you can learn from. Eventually, you build experience and relationships and make friends, and that's how you improve."

BD's story encapsulates several of the skills discussed throughout these pages. He hustled, showed up, learned the ropes, and kept improving. Any skills he lacked, he pushed himself to practice and learn, over and over, until he was comfortable. He looked for every opportunity and put himself out there. Those are the qualities that made him a successful actor in an industry that is as cutthroat as it gets. CodeBreaking came naturally to him, and he's teaching the value of these qualities to other game changers.

Believe

We can be our own worst enemies when it comes to believing what is possible for our lives. Naysayers don't help and can keep us paralyzed and second-guessing what we are capable of. At the risk of sounding cliché, the only person who stands in the way of you accomplishing your goals is you. Become who you believe you are.

I believe your unique skillset is directly connected to the dream you have for your life. If you open your mind to the potential, with effort and perseverance, you can CodeBreak your way into any arena you want. The missed opportunities are only an issue when you don't take the shot. It's not about winning each and every shot. If you take enough shots, even with your missing ingredients, eventually you will win.

The CodeBreaker Mindset™ Takeaways

- Be highly competent and prepared. It's just the price of admission.
- Focus on what you have, not on what you don't.
- Be willing to put yourself out there, even when it's uncomfortable.
- Own who you are and your strengths. Start building a brand around it.
- Repel anyone else's FOBD.
- Hustle wins.

Chapter 11

Creating Ecosystems and Network Effects

> Meaningful relationships are invaluable for building and sustaining a culture of excellence, because they create the trust and support that people need to push each other to do great things.[48]
>
> —Ray Dalio, Founder of Bridgewater Associates

We've all heard the adage, "It's not what you know, it's who you know." It's irrefutable; networking is a significant element in finding success in business and life. Some even argue it's the most significant. While you might have a skill or product that is light-years ahead of anything else in the market, you simply can't make it a success by yourself. These pages will equip you with differentiated strategies to create virtuous, progressive ecosystems and network effects.

At this stage in the evolution of our planet, Earth, building relationships is a normal practice. Humans are, for the most part, social beings. Whether in school, career, volunteering, local communities, etc., we find ourselves making various levels of relationships with acquaintances, colleagues, friends, and family members.

We build relationships in defined ways, which is good and necessary for survival. Do we think about our relationships in the context of building ecosystems and network effects? Do we look for patterns, synergies, and concentrations of characteristics while also understanding the linear and, more importantly, nonlinear benefits that can arise?

Relationships

CASE STUDY

Mindy Grossman, Consello, Partner and Vice Chair; Fanatics, Board Member; Former CEO of WW

Mindy Grossman is a three-time CEO wonder in the consumer and retail industry. She has been CEO of WW (formerly Weight Watchers), a publicly traded company with media icon Oprah Winfrey as a significant shareholder; Home Shopping Network, Inc. (HSNi), spinning it out and taking it public from another media titan, Barry Diller's IAC; and CEO of Polo Jeans Company for legendary designer Ralph Lauren. She's also held pivotal leadership roles at iconic brands such as IAC, Nike, Ralph Lauren, and Tommy Hilfiger. Currently, she's Partner and Vice Chair at Consello, an advisory and investing platform, while also serving as a board member for various companies, including Michael Rubin's sports platform Fanatics.

Mindy has a reputation for working with global titans and deep credibility in the consumer and retail industries. When asked about her success, Mindy says, "I am, at my core, a relationship person. One of the elements of my having success has been the relationships I've built across industries, across businesses, for almost forty-eight years."

Authentic

"Relationship can be one of those overused words," Mindy explains. "A true relationship needs to be authentic. You both need to respect one another and have mutual trust. You know the relationship is true if you're able to have conversations that feel like what I call 'productive discomfort.' Because having hard conversations is part of it. You have to build ultimate trust to be able to work together, build teams together, build culture together, and have the results lead to business success.

"One of the other major assets of leadership, when you're thinking of relationship building, is to cultivate an innate curiosity about others and not stay in your own bubble. I joke around that I was totally not qualified for the role of running HSNi because I had no television experience, no media experience, no experience in most of the businesses that HSNi was in, because apparel was only a portion of it. I didn't understand the idea of channels and networks, but I knew what the consumer would want, and I could work backward from there. But that's also how it is with building relationships. It's not just people that you want in your aura. It's building relationships with every group of stakeholders that you'll interact with. That's what both builds your brand and helps those relationships."

Be Curious About Finding New Intersections

Reaching out to people we're curious about begins by seeing value in connecting with others who are different from us, in learning something new, or in having a unique and personal adventure. Do we go places that, on the surface, appear not to be "our kind of place"? Just because something doesn't immediately appear to "fit" our interests, doesn't mean it won't introduce us to someone new who could be a positive addition to our lives.

Life moves fast, and given the agents of chaos, we can tend to veer to our conscious and subconscious biases. Everybody does this. When we only go to places we're familiar with, we never put ourselves into novel intersections or ecosystems to meet different people. Often, when we do go to events, we stick to talking to people we know.

We may be less inclined to say hello to the stranger and spend time specifically meeting those whom we've never met, who look different than us, or sound different than us. Those who seem to be quite opposite. In the drive for efficiency, we may over-filter out possibilities and additive interludes.

Build Networks Across Different Platforms and Industries

One of Mindy's weekly commitments is to either meet someone she's never met before or to experience something for the first time. She also puts herself in new intersections and encourages others to do the same. At HSNi, being new to the beauty business, Mindy says, "I joined a number of groups in that sector. At one point, I had to deliver a fireside chat at one of the big events, and I was talking about how every sector affects the others. I asked the room, 'How many people in this room have been to the Consumer Electronics Show?' This was in 2008–2009, and nobody raised their hand. I said, 'The biggest disruption in beauty is going to come from technology.' Fast forward, and that's a lot of what has happened today. You have to think about getting out of your lane and having many different experiences so you can build networks across different platforms and industries."

Be conscious and intentional not to succumb to the status quo of life, which includes the status quo of relationship building, and instead open yourself to thinking and acting differently. You may be thinking, *Okay, CEOs and leaders can do this, but what about me?* Let's explore some new practices for how to engage people and rebound if things feel off.

If You Don't Go, How Will You Know?

If you don't put yourself in new intersections, you won't know who you can meet. What beautiful moment, person, lesson, observation, or growth did you miss out on because you did not venture into that new space?

Here's a practical application. When there are conferences or events based on gender or affinity groups, do you go even if you don't identify with that specific group? Unless the event has explicit statements on who can or cannot attend the event, why not go? You'll stand out, and that can be a good thing.

As an alumna of HBS, I attended a conference the school hosted to celebrate the fiftieth anniversary of the African-American Student Union. The conference was open not only to African-American alumni, but any alumni, student, or non-Harvard affiliated person could attend. The agenda was packed with sessions where participants could learn from CEO and C-Suite African-American leaders from Fortune 500 companies, investors, and the business community on commercial topics.

I went and met an attendee who was a South Asian male alum of HBS. As I looked around, it struck me that more people of other backgrounds had not attended.

He said, "With all these heavy-hitter leaders speaking right in my backyard of Boston, I wouldn't miss it. I didn't have to take a plane; I just had to drive to campus. I want to meet new people, learn about what's going on in different industries, and gain intel on career, advisor, or board opportunities."

Another point of surprise for me was that more students on campus, where the conference took place mere footsteps away from their dormitories, did not attend. The event was open to everyone. As a student, regardless of how you identify racially, ethnically, etc., if you're looking for a job or want to start putting your name out there, why not go? You could meet an alum of the school and ask if they'll mentor you. Even in the rare instance where you don't talk to anyone, you will at least gain knowledge and insights from top leaders.

Remember, nine times out of ten, you will not regret showing up. Also, consider that by going, you're giving serendipity the opportunity to appear and work in your favor. All you have to do is take a chance and go. If you decide not to attend and succumb to the many easy reasons to stay at home, you, by default, take yourself off the game's playing field.

Create the Best Energy for a Connection

When launching into the first dialogue, what's the best way to come across as open and warm? Here are a few pieces of advice I remind myself of when I want to make a positive impression.

Be a Giver

What you give is what you attract. This is the law of attraction, where "positive thoughts bring positive results into a person's life. A positive mindset will attract more success and happiness than a negative one."[49] When you meet a person, do you engage with the intention of what you can offer the other person? For the most part, people are attracted to the positive. Coming across as a giver, and not a taker, is one of the best ways to emanate welcoming, open, and positive energy.

Beware, though, there are takers. These types tend to be transactional and only consider talking to you after they've sized you up. They calculate who and what they perceive you to be, and if engaging with you could possibly benefit them.

People can tell when someone comes across as a taker. They are less likely to be motivated to talk to you and reveal any truth and substance of who they really are. The mistake you make in being a taker is missing the gift in the person before you. Takers have yet to learn that everyone has something to offer that's waiting to be discovered. Give your attention and kindness to that person, and you may be surprised by what they share in return.

In an interaction with a high-profile person, you may wonder what you could possibly give them. Most everyone, even high-profile individuals, responds to a compliment, comment of appreciation, or thoughtful question. Be interested in who they are and what they're doing. Don't minimize yourself. That important person wants to hear what you have to say.

Practice Abundance Thinking

We succeed in teams, groups, and ecosystems. When you fully realize what your natural gift is (and isn't), you won't feel threatened when meeting other achievers. Manage down feelings of scarcity and fear. Use positive self-talk. Athletes do it all the time. Research has found that positive self-talk, especially when scripted and practiced beforehand, can improve confidence and positively affect performance.[50] You are in that room for a reason. You're not an impostor. You have value to offer.

Know the Stakes of the Room

Do your homework to understand who will be in the room, including any business, cultural, or social nuances. The more high-profile the room, the more nuanced the interactions can be in terms of how you present yourself and weave through sparking conversations that birth a handshake or a hello into a new relationship.

Research and Triangulate

In chapter 8, we learned about the importance of researching and triangulating data. This also applies when meeting people, networking, and building ecosystems. Research the attendees and speakers at the gathering. Reflect, analyze, and triangulate. Determine who you are interested in talking to and for what purpose (no purpose is okay too). Look up attendees' biographies, recent news, social media, or any affiliations they have.

You're looking for interests you both share. Having these details will help you with your conversation starters and elevator pitch. Triangulate to figure out who and what are transactional interludes versus relationships that can be developed into fruitful, virtuous, substantive ecosystems.

Be Prepared and Aware of How You Show Up

Be prepared and ready to dive at an opportunity. Whether you have time to prepare or it's an impromptu occasion, be intentional and focused with your mindset, thoughts, and actions. Present yourself as polished and put together. Have your emotional intelligence or EQ turned on. If these are not your strong suits, seek out learning and coaching to work on these areas.

Have your elevator pitch and multiple versions of it ready, depending on who you are talking to. Own it. Be confident. Practice in the mirror if that helps. Arm yourself with conversation starters in advance if that helps you to be at ease to engage.

Seek Feedback to Understand How You Show Up

How do others receive you in a networking environment? Be available to receive feedback and reflect on the networking interactions later to see what adjustments you may want to make in your approach and style. You want data-driven feedback and, in certain situations, perception-driven feedback. In chapter 8, we cautioned on perception-driven feedback, but it's useful as one source of intel because it can reveal how people are receiving you. Determine if you agree or disagree with those perceptions, and let it inform how you choose to operate and present yourself when you are "working" the room.

Even dealing with people in a networking and social environment is a game, and you are always navigating against others' insecurities and scarcity mindsets. Seek feedback from peers, those junior or senior to you, bosses, professional coaches, etc.

Learn How to Adjust Yourself When You're Not Clicking with Someone, but Only to a Point

When you meet someone, do you ever feel unsure if you are clicking with them? This can often happen if we feel any level of intimidation or insecurity, justified or unjustified, in the interaction with the other person. Calling this out here makes you aware. If you are aware, you can then pause in the moment. Be conscious and determine how you want to pivot in the dialogue to try to resonate with the person. Try to warm the person up. However, if the conversation does not seem to be resonating, that's okay. Let it politely conclude.

By all means, you can adjust yourself however much you feel comfortable with to connect with the other person. If the vibe is not there, that's okay. If you don't want to adjust yourself, that is fine too. You can only adjust yourself to the point when something stops feeling right, or until you reach so far that it feels like you're behaving in a way that is not your true self. You can only subdue or contort yourself for so long before your true self starts peeking through the façade. There are more than eight billion people on the planet, and you are not going to get along with every one of them.

If a conversation or situation is going to be sustainable for you, it's got to be from a place where you can be who you are—a place where your superpower, the secret sauce that makes you, *you*, is welcomed. Like Dr. David Thomas, Morehouse College, President, said in chapter 9, go where you're with people who see you the way you see yourself.

Bridge the Gap with Others If You Can

CASE STUDY

Ndidi Okonkwo Nwuneli, ONE Campaign, President and CEO

Ndidi Okonkwo Nwuneli, President and CEO of ONE Campaign, is no stranger to putting herself in high-altitude, diverse spheres and figuring out how to connect with those who are different than her. With roots in Nigeria, Ndidi has been globally recognized and awarded for her leadership and impact in social entrepreneurship and international development across Africa. This has included founding LEAP Africa, a nonprofit that developed African leaders and food changemakers, to then launching AACE Foods, which democratized the supply of food from ten thousand–plus farmers and provided access to food for Africans.

Ndidi was recruited by global icon Bono (lead singer of U2), Aliko Dangote (CEO of the multi-billion-dollar conglomerate Dangote Industries Limited), and other distinguished leaders to the ONE Campaign. The organization "exists to create a more just and equal world" through solutions and "policies to reduce inequality and global poverty, improve economic and food security," and expand access to healthcare, education, and employment.[51]

Your Own Merit

Ndidi took me into her experiences of bridging the gap with others. "People expect you to behave a certain way because you look a certain way, and you have that extra burden. I had an extra burden early in life because I looked very young. You walk into a room, it doesn't matter where in Africa, there's tremendous ageism, right? Because people respect the elders. It's a great part of our culture, but if you're a young entrepreneur and you're female, you have a burden of proof. I learned this skill in McKinsey [& Company], where I started my career, that you have the first five minutes of a meeting to determine whether you're an influencer in that meeting or whether you're irrelevant. So, how you show up matters. I have had to teach other young people and my team members how to make themselves visible by bringing brilliant insights, questions, and comments into every room they step into to prove themselves and their worth, so they don't say, 'Who's that young woman? She's just filling a quota. We needed a youth voice. We needed a woman's voice.' But by the time you're done with that interaction, you've convinced them that you really earned this. You deserve to be here on your own merit."

Take the Shot. Be Okay with Missed Shots.

Sometimes people choke. They circle . . . they eye . . . and they may even go up to the person, but they do not take their shot. Or they start and fumble. I get it; this is not easy. Practice makes perfect. Just as we discussed about building muscle memory in chapter 6, the only way you rise to proficiency at networking is to take your shot. Sometimes you will land. Sometimes you won't. There is no such thing as rejection, only missed opportunities. If you don't click with the other person, it is a learning experience to know your energy may not be aligned with theirs. Or perhaps it was not aligned in that moment. You can then determine if you want to try again in the future and, if so, how many times.

Rejection Is Redirection

On rejection, Mindy Grossman says, "If there's something you're passionate about, why not pursue it? Too many people don't have the self-belief to do that. I'm okay with rejection, because in a lot of cases, it moves you forward and gives you opportunity."

Building on her point, if you're a CodeBreaker, take as many shots as you can, not worrying about what other people think. If you miss the shot or if the other person rejects you, who cares? There is more value in you taking the shot because of the learning opportunities and possibilities that may arise if you click with the other person.

Opportunity Knocks—Be Ready

We've talked about how important it is to be prepared. The key to successful networking is the ability to move quickly when opportunities present themselves. If your reaction is delayed, the opportunity may pass you by.

For instance, are you ready if the connection you've been dying to get some face time with gets on the elevator with you? What if you had this person alone for the time it took to ride up four floors? Could you get your thoughts out coherently in a persuasive pitch? Could you offer them enough to entertain a follow-up call? If you're even the slightest bit unsure, then your homework is to concentrate on refining your pitch.

Why is it worth doing all this preparation ahead of time? Have the talking points or some ideas in your head because you never know when you will run into the person. Be intentional. If you are prepared, then you will be less caught off guard, and your muscle memory will kick in and enable you to let the conversation flow.

When you lay the groundwork for any relationship, it helps to build a rapport with them. A brief "Hello" can become a short "How are you?" which can evolve into more. Seeing the person multiple times, even if briefly, creates familiarity and puts the other person at ease, increasing the ability to speak to each other. Remember, my initial meeting with the national award–winning journalist Soledad O'Brien at the conference was quick and rushed (see chapter 7). Months later, in New York, when we ran into each other, she remembered our brief meeting, and it made her more open to having an impromptu conversation. You may only get one shot with a person, so make sure you're ready.

The Art of Small Talk

In a world full of immediate gratification junkies, deals can be made or broken in a matter of minutes. Few people have much of an attention span anymore. Be ready to make it quick and good.

Technology has provided the world with incredible advances, but has also reduced our face-to-face engagements. Making in-person connections, once common, has been replaced by dating apps, people working from home, and holding meetings through online conferencing platforms. Our interactions with each other rely more on clicking "like" or sending an emoji than on having live human interactions. But a big part of networking relies on going old-school and making impromptu connections with others at a conference, event, or in a serendipitous moment on the subway. So let's take some time to brush up on how to start a conversation with someone you've never met.

When you walk into the conference, event, or down the street, what do you do when you run into, for example, the CEO of Starbucks? You've already thought about them at some point in your consciousness because you've jumped on Google and done some sleuthing. You know enough to recognize them, their name, and title. You should already have something in your mind on how to make a connection.

Here's how the interaction could go:

You: *Hi, it's a nice day. How are you? Aren't you the CEO of Starbucks? Nice to meet you. What made you decide to speak at this conference?* Or, *Thank you so much for offering so many tea options—I'm not a coffee drinker.*

You may think this sounds silly to the other person, or even to you, but it doesn't.

Now, the door is open, and the ball is in their court on whether and how to engage in the conversation. Another option is to ask, "What brings you to this event?" Even if you don't have anything brilliant to say, the mere fact that you're both located in a common physical place provides a conversation starter.

If the idea of doing this makes you nervous and you feel stuck at the art of conversation, find resources to help you. Whether taking a class, reading relevant literature on the topic, or scoring tips from friends, family, or colleagues. Even practicing in front of the mirror or role-playing with a friend can help you grow more comfortable. Try it out with the cashier at the grocery store or dry cleaners. Practice and repetition will get you more comfortable talking with strangers. You're sharpening a critical life skill that will help you advance.

This is also where having emotional intelligence or EQ can serve you well. When you're chatting up the person, listen closely and read their reaction. If you're feeling alignment, you might not need to rush, so slow it down and monitor the pace and intensity of the flow of dialogue. The conversation may be self-propelling, mutual, and enjoyable.

Prioritize

You may have a limited or unknown amount of time at the gathering to meet those you are interested in. Have a plan for how you want to spend your time and who you want to approach. You may have a certain order in which you would like to talk to people. If that order does not work out, be ready for impromptu or serendipitous opportunities, which are often at play in any encounter. If you have a person, or two, or three, who are a must for you to talk to, then focus on them. Don't lollygag. Don't assume, *Hey, I will catch the person before they leave.* You don't know what their plans are. If you see an opening, take it. If you don't get an easy opening, make a plan for how you will politely glide your way into introducing yourself to the person.

Prioritizing also helps you achieve a return on investment on your time, energy, and bandwidth. You're not wandering around the event or networking aimlessly. You're moving with purpose, whether that's to learn, grow career- or business-wise, or have fun.

Positive Connections

Why do some people resonate and some don't?

Sometimes, you resonate with another person because you have something in common. Both of you might be female or Canadian. Maybe you went to the same school or worked at the same company. You may have shared values, styles, or frames of reference. Of course, having things in common doesn't mean you will automatically click.

Another reason may be that the person is very different from you—in gender, culture, or religion. It's important to put out positive energy and effort every time you meet a person. You never know when you'll hit it off with someone. Sometimes, the person you think will be an automatic vibe is not, and you have to spend more time getting to know them. Other times, the person you think you have nothing in common with is the person you were meant to meet, and it turns into a great friendship. That's why it's important to always put your best foot forward. Focus on the substance of the person and interaction, regardless of your initial perception and feelings.

Negative Vibrations and Dealing with Rejection

Crabs at the Christmas Party

Early in my career, at an annual Christmas party, I approached the CEO of the company and told him I'd heard a speech he'd made at another event and how, as a woman of color, it made me feel I belonged. Later, at the same party, the CEO found me, touched me on the shoulder, and said, "I appreciated your comment, and, yes, there is a place for you here." (This is what a good leader does.)

A short time later, while still at the party, some of the managing directors who had witnessed this leaned over to me and frowned. "We saw the CEO talking to you. What were you talking about?" They said it in a way that made it clear that I wasn't supposed to do that. I did not realize that it was not the cultural norm for a mid-level professional to approach the CEO and have a conversation.

Afterward, these colleagues started to make my life difficult in meetings. People would make comments like "You manage up really well." They were implying I was not a team player. I internalized these comments, and it began to undermine my confidence. Should I not speak to the CEO anymore? Should I do it privately, not in public, where other people could see? I overthought it, grew more stressed, and developed self-doubt.

As time went on, I started avoiding other senior-level team members. If they approached me, I'd quickly end the conversation. I was afraid other people would see me, and it would be viewed as me "managing up." I also started feeling awkward. I was sabotaging myself and did not even realize it, much less knew what to do about it.

Then one day, when I was exiting the cafeteria, I rode the escalator with a member of senior leadership. He said, "Hey, I saw you at that event. You didn't even say hi."

I was careful with my response. "I didn't want to take up your time. I'm sure you're busy talking to other, more important people."

He turned to me. "Sure, but these events are for us to interact with everybody. So, you should talk to people."

"Oh, I've gotten feedback in the past that I shouldn't talk to senior management," I responded.

He said, "Well, I don't know who's giving you that feedback, but that's not good advice." Something clicked. He was right. I wasn't the one with the problem; it was the other people. Their behavior represented their insecurity and a level of toxicity.

They were the crabs in the bucket. You've heard about the crabs, right? "[The] 'crab mentality' reflects an attitude that prefers dragging others down rather than seeing them rise up. Crabs in a bucket will pull down any crab that tries to escape, ensuring no one achieves freedom. Similarly, people with a crab mentality resent the success of others and try to undermine them."[52] The world is full of "leaders" and people like this. They make you a basket case.

Leaders should want to see their staff talking to the CEO. Knowing how to interact and talk to senior people is part of the criteria for moving up the ranks. It certainly shouldn't be held against you. A secure manager would have said something like, "Good for you for talking with the CEO. I'm glad you took the initiative. What did you learn? Awesome. You should cultivate that in the future and reach out to him again in six months." As leaders, we should want to develop our team's talent.

There will be energy misalignment sometimes; it's part of life. Keep it moving. Don't let it hurt or debilitate your confidence. You don't have time for mean people, bullies, or snobs. There are more than eight billion people on the planet. Find your tribe. There's one more thing you can do to help yourself . . .

Learn from It

If you lack alignment with a person, no stress. We're not trying to give anybody mental health issues from trying to connect with someone who doesn't want it or is not willing. What can you learn from it?

Mindy Grossman had this to add when dealing with rejection. "It's never comfortable, so you have to get comfortable with discomfort. The question you have to ask yourself is, Why did the person reject me? Is it just that they didn't have time? Or was it just something they couldn't consume at that point, or didn't seem relevant to them? I think it's good to do the work of sitting back to understand. Was there something you could have done differently or not? Then you just have to move on. You can't dwell. Dwell is not a good word."

When things don't go well, I make it a point to do a postmortem, reflecting on whether it was an outside factor or if I could have done something differently. Another tip is to call a friend and give them the rundown—get their input.

Keep in mind, how a person experiences you has far less to do with you and far more to do with them. These are some signals to be mindful of when interacting with others:

- Are they secure or insecure with themselves?
- Are they independent and objective-minded, or not?
- Are they open to people who have different experiences and backgrounds?
- How much conscious or subconscious bias do they have?

- Do they have a scarcity mindset or an abundance mindset?
- Are they data-, perception-, or manipulation-driven? (See chapter 8.)

For all the above signals, you may not know with certainty, especially for people who are new to you. Your informed intuition (see chapter 7) may provide indications. Real data, through multiple or substantive interactions, will corroborate or dispute your early assessment.

Build Your Ecosystems. Dogs Don't Bark at Parked Cars.

A mentor of mine, a former Premier of a province in Canada, told me, "Dogs don't bark at parked cars." If people are barking, it means you are doing something right, something they care about. There's a high probability that you are doing something good, so rock on. Don't succumb to anyone hating on you for building ecosystems.

Some view networking as a bad thing. They mischaracterize and mis-criticize those who want to climb the ladder. This is a misnomer. Are we put on Earth to move down in life? No, we are here to progress. You've heard the adage: If you're not growing, you're dying. People will say whatever they want, especially criticism or "haterism," out of their own insecurity, scarcity mindset, and conscious and/or subconscious biases. Don't worry about what other people think or how others are perceiving you working the room.

Haters are hanging on every lamppost, but now you're more equipped to spot them when they try to block your light. Know how to switch them off and unplug their power.

Virtuous Flywheels and Ecosystems of Intelligence

The agents of chaos have changed the stickiness and longevity of relationships, as we explored in chapter 1. In your personal or professional life, bi-directional relationships are still important. However, it is more important than ever to have multi-pronged relationships in intersections with hyper-connectivity, whether you are the connector in that ecosystem, or you are connected to whoever is the connector. This is true both online and in person.

LinkedIn is an example of a massive ecosystem where members can connect and see how many connections they have in common. The more connections you have may be a signal that shared values and interests exist to give birth to substantive online and, more importantly, real-life relationships. This is similarly true for professional membership organizations and school alumni associations.

Network Effects

Real competitive advantage is created and discovered through cultivating ecosystems of intelligence. Whether the common denominator is industry, company, functional role, geography, or any interest area, seeding virtuous circles that you can tap for ideas, feedback, and collaboration will always be a winning approach. Technology and AI have only made the race for the best and most unique creative and execution abilities paramount.

Developing those ecosystems that house competency concentrations around any characteristics or expertise areas you value creates a competitive network effect and advantage. Virtuous flywheels and ecosystems of thought leadership and community, as well as commercial and monetizable opportunities, are a winning model for longevity. For example, in a business or commercial context, revenue growth and acceleration are not only about who you can sell to in a bi-directional, binary way, but about orchestrating a compounding network effect. Thus, it takes an active, enduring strategy to align the interests and incentives of multiple diverse stakeholders, in order to sell to, with, and through other actors in the ecosystem.

Another benefit of finding groups and intersections of shared relationships is that it enables others to validate and cross-reference you. This has become even more important with the proliferation of the second agent of chaos, the breakdown of reliable data. Less and less information, whether words or images, is independently verifiable. This breeds more distortion and distrust. With all the noise and the increase in people subconsciously programmed to skim and swipe on social media rather than explicitly read, analyze, and think, people's ability to discern is decreasing and deteriorating rapidly.

To compensate for this, people may come across as not able to immediately digest verifiable data right before their eyes, or find it suspicious or less likely to believe that which is real. They may then seek confirmation and validation of you through quick internet searches, particularly on social media, and by polling their network to see who knows you. As we talked about in chapter 8, this may not be a good thing, depending on whether they are relying on perception- or manipulation-driven information versus data-driven.

The Reference Check

Take, for example, the old-fashioned reference check. Several decades ago, if someone wanted to do a reference check, they could easily call or write to someone in your local city or community. Now, especially in a global, digital, and social media–driven world, the ability to reference check can be opaque. People are looking for multiple sources of intel on who you are, what you've done, and who you know. They may analyze and cross-reference all the inputs, often quickly, to formulate their view on a person, even if the inputs are quick sound bites from others, or a flash of images on the internet and social media. The big caution is that they may not pause to even question or verify the integrity of the input sources. Thus, the more people in a particular intersection know you or have some sense of you, they *may* help when you are reference checked.

Having access, especially to the best and brightest or those "in the know," will add value in any dimension of life. Being a part of ecosystems relevant to you is a way for you to achieve enrichment, productivity, effectiveness, and, hopefully, enjoyment from relationships.

The CodeBreaker Mindset™ Takeaways

- If you don't go, how will you know? Seize opportunities to venture into new spaces to meet new and diverse people.
- Be prepared. Have your conversation starters and elevator pitch ready. Keep it succinct, effective, and impactful.
- Be confident that you belong in that room and have something valuable to add to the conversation.
- Look for patterns in intersections and groups to locate, cultivate, and compound network effects and ecosystems of intelligence.
- Dogs don't bark at parked cars!

PART III

Victorious CodeBreaker

Chapter 12

Study the Outliers

> Outliers are those who have been given opportunities—and who have had the strength and presence of mind to seize them.[53]
>
> —Malcolm Gladwell, award-winning author

What Is an Outlier?

An outlier is a statistical observation that is markedly different in value from the others in the sample.[54] When describing a person as an outlier, it means someone who is atypical within a particular group, class, or category.[55] In other words, outliers are unconventional, anomalies, nonconformists, or those sometimes referred to as long shots. They often aren't part of the crowd, and they achieve their positions in nonlinear ways.

For example, the entertainment industry makes billions showcasing outlier or unicorn personalities. Hollywood movies about a person who defies the odds, slays the dragon, saves the world, or finds success by going against the grain become the next blockbuster. Books about people who share their story of an unconventional path to the top often hit the best-seller lists. It is largely the outliers who carry the most credit for advances in any industry.

Outliers offer you a window into the edge of innovation, the future at scale, new and emerging processes, systems, technologies, products, and services, as well as fresh ways of thinking, being, and doing. A critical part of The CodeBreaker Mindset™ is spotting signals and trends, and then evaluating what to act on. Whether it is hunting your vision to reality or pivoting yourself before others do, the person who can see where things are going ahead of time and acts on that will win. Building this observation and analytical muscle is what studying outliers will reward us with. This chapter will fly into how developing actionable pattern recognition from outliers will power you with a competitive advantage.

Outliers Fall Outside of the Normal Distribution

How is it possible for someone to exist on the edge of the same world as you, not follow the typical path, yet still manage to find success? Is it by design? By luck? It's both, as well as other factors, which we'll explore in this chapter.

In a group, outliers stand out because they think and behave differently. Because of this, they may be seen as a problem or a novelty. Outliers tend to roam in filtered ecosystems because their differences can make it challenging to connect and relate with others. Highly proficient in some areas, the outlier may present deficiencies in other areas.

Where do outliers fit in The CodeBreaker Mindset™? All outliers are CodeBreakers, but not all CodeBreakers are outliers. In the diagram, the gray part represents CodeBreakers. The white striped circle indicates outliers. The conclusion is that only a small fraction of CodeBreakers are outliers.

Not All CodeBreakers Are Outliers

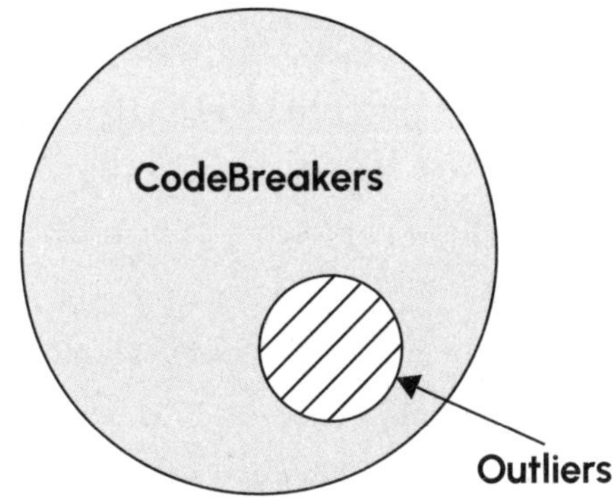

A small portion of CodeBreakers are outliers.

Whether you are an outlier or not, you can identify, study, and learn from them to increase your understanding of the written and unwritten rules, pivots, and serendipity involved in pursuing goals. Today's outlier may mature and receive mass market adoption and implementation in the future, making it the new status quo. Let's bring this to life by examining the discovery story of a global entertainment superstar.

Justin Bieber: Breaking Through

Every budding artist craves being discovered. Shows like *America's Got Talent*, *American Idol*, and *The Voice* prove that sometimes all a person needs is one big break.

Over the last couple of decades, using social media to showcase talent and expertise, build a brand, and market oneself to audiences and stakeholders has become a common practice. But this wasn't always the case. In the late 1990s, during the early days of social media, much of society was skeptical about using it, uncertain if it would survive.[56] This became the case even more so when people tried to use social media for sales and marketing.

In 2007, a twelve-year-old from Stratford, Ontario, Canada, named Justin Bieber "uploaded his first video to YouTube with the help of Pattie, his mother. The clip was grainy, and Bieber's tiny frame was a mere silhouette moving around a dimly lit church stage. But the quality of the video didn't matter; the real star of the video was Bieber's voice. It was undeniable, a big and bellowing presence as he reached for the high notes of Ne-Yo's song, 'So Sick.'"[57]

"YouTube was in its infancy, barely two years old, when Bieber started posting his performance videos. He covered Lil Bow Wow, Sarah McLachlan, and Alicia Keys. At the time, YouTube was considered a playground for amateur home-video experimentation, not the birthplace of pop stars. Not even Bieber was looking for fame there."[58]

Necessary and Accidental Outliers

During his first appearance on *The Ellen Show*, Bieber explained, "I was in a singing competition a while back. I was twelve years old, and my friends and family that couldn't make it wanted to see me, so I posted those videos on YouTube, and I guess it just kind of blew up."[59] The way that Bieber exploded, though, was a first in so many ways.

Architected Outlier

Music executive Scooter Braun "discovered Bieber's videos on YouTube . . . [He] had ideas of using YouTube to break [out] an artist by making video content, and everyone said, 'You can't take an artist off YouTube and make them into a star.' "[60]

Scooter Braun teamed up with music superstar Usher, and they signed Justin Bieber in 2008. In 2009, Justin Bieber released his first album, *My World*, which peaked at number 5 on the *Billboard* 200.[61] The rest is history: "Justin Bieber has gone on to become one of the best-selling music artists of all time."[62]

Nonlinear Success

Justin Bieber's nontraditional journey to superstardom makes him an outlier. Compare and contrast Bieber's path with "the Katy Perrys and Taylor Swifts, musicians who had been discovered through more traditional means of relocating to big cities first and performing at industry showcases."[63]

The path to success is not singular or linear for most successful musicians—in fact, it isn't singular or linear for most professions, industries, or opportunities. If you examine those around you whom you aspire to be, you will see trends of non-homogeneity and uniqueness in their journey. If you zoom in on the stretch dimensions of their life, you may see outlier attributes and behaviors. There can be patterns of inputs, written and unwritten rules, processes, methodologies, and various approaches that can be drawn upon to inform your pattern recognition as you craft your steps forward. However, like with many career or life pursuits, the road to success is individualized.

Unintentional Outlier

In the case of Justin Bieber, his path was a significant and historic outlier for that time. He was not looking to get discovered. His mom simply posted the video so their family and friends could see his performance at the church. This was also a pivot from analog technology (watching Bieber's performance in person) to digital (seeing it on YouTube).

The Role of Serendipity in Outliers

Scooter Braun accidentally clicked on Justin Bieber's performance on YouTube and watched it. This is both an unintentional and a serendipitous tailwind.

In addition, Scooter Braun had a thesis to create artist content, put it on YouTube, and use that to break out an artist by getting them views, with a goal of going viral. His outlier approach began with an intentional strategy.

However, randomly finding an extraordinarily gifted voice in Justin Bieber was serendipitous, and skyrocketing this next music sensation using YouTube was anything but the status quo.

Outliers Evolve into the Status Quo

The methods used by Justin Bieber, Scooter Braun, and their team created a new blueprint that is now used across professions and industries to get eyes on the next thing, be it the latest talent, gadget, or a new and improved service. Over time, leveraging YouTube and social media has become a well-established sales and distribution channel for businesses to showcase and sell their products and services at scale to global audiences.

Many societal norms have started from outlier behaviors, like going to school. When you study the history of getting an education, it was relatively novel, even more so for females in some cultures. In 1957, a census report showed only 10 percent of Americans had a high school diploma. By 1980, 70 percent had either already earned a high school diploma or were working toward it. The same happened with college enrollment. While it was only 43 percent in 1970, it skyrocketed to around 70 percent by 2015.

The more you study the ingredients that go into outliers, whether their behaviors, pivots, serendipity, etc., the more you will be able to see linkages in the occurrence of those same ingredients in broader commercial, professional, and life strategies. Think about it: Which outlier do you know of that has stayed an outlier forever? There's an inevitable natural progression from either novelty to norm or dissolution. The faster you can translate and apply the pattern recognition gained from studying outlier attributes into your CodeBreaker Mindset™, the sharper you will become in augmenting your innovation and operating models to get ahead in business, career, and life.

Early Adopter

CASE STUDY

Tory Burch, Tory Burch LLC, Founder, Executive Chairman, Chief Creative Officer

The iconic, globally renowned and award-winning designer and entrepreneur Tory Burch prides herself on being ahead of the curve. It's how she has built a twenty-plus-year successful, enduring, global luxury brand. "Being an early adopter was critical. It wasn't really a strategy; I was going with my instincts. In 2004, everything about my business plan was counterintuitive: We were direct-to-consumer, we had multiple categories, and we launched with e-commerce—even though people kept telling me 'No one will ever shop online . . .'"

Purpose Driven

"We were also purpose driven. It was in my business plan from day one: I wanted to build a global lifestyle brand that would support a foundation for women entrepreneurs. Not everyone understood my vision for a hybrid model; a few investors even told me to never use 'business' and 'social responsibility' in the same sentence. But I wanted to prove that doing good is good for business—and today, it's gratifying that businesses aren't innovative without purpose.

"Purpose makes us a better company, and I hope we can be a role model for others in making purpose part of the bottom line."

Change Before You See It in the Numbers

When it comes to the speed of developing pattern recognition of the necessary ingredients and orchestration to build and scale profitable high-end fashion and retail companies, Tory says, "There have been so many challenges; I often say every day is like whack-a-mole. You solve one problem, and another pops up.

"Pierre-Yves [Roussel, the CEO of Tory Burch] and I talk a lot about changing before you have to, before you see it in the numbers. Otherwise, it's too late; meaningful change takes time. When he joined in 2019, I was able to rethink everything about our collections; I redesigned every product we make and began taking our aesthetic in a new direction. People think it happened overnight, but it was many years in the works. We're still on our journey of reinvention, and I've never felt more excited about what I do."

Independent Thinkers, Creators, and Operators

Galileo Galilei, the Italian astronomer, physicist, and engineer, is credited with sparking the birth of what we know as modern astronomy.[64] He was the first to use a telescope to record observations of the night sky. The first to discover that the moon's surface was not flat, but full of many geological formations like Earth. He also realized Jupiter had moons orbiting it, which helped solidify his heliocentric theory.[65] His theories, though empirical, were dismissed by the Roman Catholic Church.

Why?

Galileo was a nonconformist at heart and didn't subscribe to the common belief that the Earth was the center of the universe. This geocentric model was based on references in the Bible, which described the sun in constant motion around the Earth. This erroneous model was also backed by Ptolemy, which shows us how common it is to rely unquestioningly on groupthink and to follow the masses, even when they are wrong.[66] When we insist on a certain belief system, a certain way of thinking, knowing, doing, and being, it allows the propagation of untruths. It leaves no room for fresh ideas.

Galileo observed that the Earth and other celestial bodies revolved around the sun, meaning the sun—not the Earth—was the center of the universe.

Galileo published his findings, but instead of being lauded for an incredible discovery, he was persecuted for his contrarian viewpoint and banned from teaching his findings. In February of 1616, he was officially exiled from the Roman Catholic Church for speaking out about his discoveries.[67]

As an outlier and independent thinker, Galileo was punished to the point of being discredited. Now, hundreds of years later, his findings have been substantiated. This is a common scenario in history when changemakers come along and disrupt the establishment. In many cases, instead of being initially celebrated, they are often resisted because many people fear change, that which they don't understand, or that which they feel poses a threat to their power, influence, and way of life. These reasons are similar to other barriers to change discussed throughout *The CodeBreaker Mindset*™ and are why society seeks to protect the status quo at all costs.

Outliers Create New Categories

As previously touched on, social media, once a new category, is now mainstream, and is widely used by many different types of businesses and entrepreneurs for brand building, marketing, selling goods and services, and conducting transactions. Social media caused the proliferation and expansion of another modern category of "influencers."

Social Media Influencers

"The term social media influencer can loosely be applied to any individual who has the capacity to incite a behavior with his or her followers (in this sense, anyone with a social media account and a following of friends and family can be deemed an influencer). But it's most commonly used to refer to individuals who have the capacity to encourage a significant group of followers to make purchasing decisions. In other words, the term often refers to individuals who are aiding with the marketing and advertising efforts—be that officially or not—of one or more organizations."[68]

Many people globally have done what Justin Bieber did and have gone on to become celebrities and influencers using social media. These self-made stars can have exclusive endorsement deals with various brands because they understand the unique reach they have on consumer preferences, consumption patterns, and buying decisions. Within a matter of a few years, some of these influencers have gone from being outliers to being known the world over for the content and sway they produce. They seized opportunities—do you?

Outlier as the Start of Something Important

CASE STUDY

Michelle Peluso, Revlon, CEO and Nike, Board Member

As a four-time CEO across multiple industries, Michelle Peluso is an outlier in her professional journey. Her first CEO appointment was in travel and hospitality at Site59 and then Travelocity. Surfing the surge of e-commerce, Michelle became CEO of Gilt Groupe, where fashion and technology intersect. Michelle excelled in leadership roles as the Chief Customer and Experience Officer at CVS Health and prior to that, the Chief Marketing Officer at IBM. Her fourth CEO role is at Revlon, the diversified beauty and fashion empire. In addition, Michelle has been a board member of Nike for more than a decade.

Trendspotting

Michelle offers her take on outliers. "You're really talking in some ways about trendspotting. How do you understand when an outlier is just an outlier versus the outlier as the start of something more important?

"There's no doubt that so many things, if I looked back five years before something became a big deal, the signs were there. That was true in social media. I remember the very early days of MySpace, and something about that was so nascent, so beginning. But something about that concept felt very powerful. We remember the early days of AI. I was at IBM, and in the archives, you're looking at when IBM Watson beat *Jeopardy*. This was before my time, but a real seminal moment for the country. It took twenty years before AI started to hit the mainstream."

At Revlon, Michelle says the team has been studying its brand, Almay. "It's an incredible brand that's been around since the 1930s. In the archives, we found an ad for Almay in the 1960s about how it was the first brand in that era to not use certain ingredients deemed not good for your skin.

"You have this magical moment where we've done all the research, know what consumers want, and then we go back to the archive, and with a lot of serendipity, here's something we've always done."

An outlier that benefited Revlon was realizing that it had a "history of being a skin first brand, sensitive skin brand, a clean brand, that's all the way back in our roots. Sometimes you can take data, serendipity, and magic and bring them together and come up with something powerful." These sensibilities and value propositions around clean and sensitive skin care matured from being novel to mainstream for many decades.

"Be open to and curious about those things that could potentially be very disruptive. That's one of the more important things when you're thinking about outliers, you really want to be focused on the things that can be truly disruptive, truly change the game. Truly break the rules as you know them. Those are the things that we want to spend more attention with as leaders."

What Can Outliers Teach Us?

Studying outliers is a wonderful way to spark creativity and generate new ideas in any industry or context, including how you formulate The Code-Breaker Mindset™ Equation (see chapter 3). Highly sought-after and filtered opportunities often involve outlier approaches.

Look for unique ingredients, behaviors, actions, or attributes, and how the outlier applied them to their success. Was the outlier birthed from a pivot, whether planned or unplanned, or a tailwind or headwind? Garner as much information as you can from outliers because it can fuel your linear and, more importantly, nonlinear pattern recognition on how to assemble, order, and orchestrate the steps to leap ahead.

Value Creation and Extraction

The parallels between Justin Bieber and Galileo are undeniable. Both were significant outliers for their time, in radically different contexts.

More so than ever, ingenuity should be embraced, but often it is squashed without a second thought. Pay attention when outliers present themselves. Especially given the agents of chaos, and technology and AI, the early indicators of the next waves of significant value creation will be in outliers. Take the long view. While the solution they're suggesting may take a major overhaul in the short term, the long-term gain will pay exponential dividends. If you believe in an idea that others find radical, don't let fear keep you from stepping outside of conformity. Put your foot in the door and distance yourself from the pack. Validation isn't necessary for you to feel the success of applying outlier behaviors. The two are not always in perfect sync. It may take some time to have confirmation that your outlier methods are working and successful. However, you may never get validation. You don't need it. Don't become discouraged. This is where you will benefit from tapping into The CodeBreaker Mindset™ Equation as the mechanism to self-validate your thoughts, plans, and decisions.

It's Tough Being an Outlier—Keep Going!

To many, the outlier is seen as an interloper or an outcast because of their unicorn thinking, operating, and being. Those who are different are often ostracized for their uniqueness.

If you are an outlier, it likely means you're the only one—or one of very few—who subscribe to unconventional thinking, and that can be lonely. It can leave you feeling unsettled or may even cause you to doubt or second-guess yourself. Not only are you alone in your beliefs, but you may also receive negative feedback and resistance from others who are unwilling to accept your ideas. It's a difficult position to be in. The important thing is that you keep going. Keep challenging the status quo. Don't give up.

The CodeBreaker Mindset™ Takeaways

- Outliers do not live as a novelty forever. Over time, they become the new norm or status quo.
- Train yourself to actively identify outliers and outlier attributes. Funnel those observations as inputs into your pattern recognition and architecture of The CodeBreaker Mindset™ Equation for business, career, and life.
- The earlier you can spot and deconstruct outliers and their attributes, the earlier you can jump ahead, especially nonlinearly, in optimizing innovation, operating, and career and life choices.

Chapter 13

Access the Force of Nature in You and Make It Happen

> My confidence offends your insecurity.[69]
>
> —Deion Sanders, two-time National Football League (NFL) Super Bowl Champion

Have you ever been told "No"?

No, you can't do that.

No, you can't go there.

No, you can't pass that test.

No, you can't get that job.

No, you can't travel.

No, you can't move to that city.

No, you can't have that boyfriend or girlfriend.

No, you can't have that friend.

No, you cannot . . .

No.

Of all the times you've been told no, did you ever ignore it? If you're a leader, with certainty, you have. There are times when we need to acquiesce and subordinate to our bosses, various stakeholders, those with power, or those who we perceive as powerful. On other occasions, we know in our bones that despite their command to stand down, we will not comply.

Everyone has a force of nature in them. Are you a breeze? A gust? A squall? Over the course of *The CodeBreaker Mindset*™, you've learned about situations that fire headwinds and those that push tailwinds. Let the storm be provoked in you. The swirling winds of the agents of chaos will only grow in intensity and velocity. If you want to resist the power of the insiders, fight atrophy and status quo thinking, and hold systems accountable for spreading manipulation-driven information, you have to elevate. Put on your armor and study the chess moves because next-level CodeBreaking is required to be a game changer.

Each one of us was born a force of nature. As a baby, we learned to sit up, roll over, crawl, stand up, and walk. Compared to tall adults, we were little creatures in an environment totally foreign to us. Yet we got back up and, through trial and error, figured out how to walk. As babies, our parents and everyone else towered over us, regularly telling us "No" or "Don't do that." How come we weren't afraid to be defiant with these large people? The baby has to be an original force of nature to acclimate and survive outside of the mother's womb.

External Headwinds Are Inevitable

You will encounter countless headwinds in your life—pre-existing structures, ecosystems, power dynamics, or exclusive clubs, each of which is designed to keep you out or down. Sharpen your EQ skills and fortitude because you'll encounter folks who will pretend to be helpful, appear to be your friend, but then snatch every opportunity to sabotage you because of their insecurity and treachery.

Headwinds can come in all shapes and sizes, regardless of how close or loving the relationship is. At the risk of sounding cynical, I've seen the fickleness of human behavior, and an apple that looks red one day can be green the next. Pay attention. Train yourself to spot when a headwind is coming. Determine how to evaluate the nature, scope, and extent of the headwind, and how you will steer. You may choose to combat or pilot through it, or take shelter until it passes. Resolve to protect your confidence and commit to not letting anything stop you.

Force of Nature (FON) Instinct

As a force of nature, it can be a delicate dance with stakeholders on how you assert yourself, yet still align with their interests and incentives, to achieve your objectives. It's also knowing how to play the game when you are told "No," and negotiating to an intersection of mutual alignment. A force of nature is equipped to outperform and outcompete its opponents. Some possess an instinct of fearlessness. Don't worry if that's not you. You can cultivate this.

Some characteristics that make a FON victorious are:

- Maniacal talent and prowess to perform and outcompete
- Strong self-confidence and self-belief
- Abundant self-love

These traits build an imaginary force field to protect your energy, mind, heart, and orbit from any *lasting* negative penetration. I say lasting because there is no denying that headwinds can have a significant impact on physical, mental, emotional, and spiritual well-being. FONs are not immune to headwinds. The difference is that they develop the know-how to repel, heal, and rebound from any resulting wounds.

In the same way that we are trained in childhood to dress for various weather possibilities by wearing the right clothing or grabbing the umbrella or snow boots, the opportunity exists to also weatherproof one's holistic being to withstand headwinds.

High-performing athletes or musicians have a similar FON mindset when it comes to practicing their craft. Real-life practice is what accumulates the knowledge, relationships, and buoyancy in one's personal bank. Build that artillery and tap into your reservoir of faith, know-how, advisors, positive self-talk, etc., to helm through any opposition.

Dealing with No

Rejection is not an anomaly; it's the norm. Many say rejection is redirection. The currents of the universe are directing us onto a different track. The quicker we can embrace the inevitability of rejection, the faster the resiliency muscle can be activated to prevent us from being debilitated. Being aware of rejection is also calibrating our mindset around the scope and magnitude of it. Not every rejection is a big thing or an ending, even if the haters and drama-seekers try to paint it that way. Evaluate in a data-driven way the true risks, outcomes, and consequences of any rejection. While something may seem major in the moment, over time, with perspective, big episodes are usually smaller than we originally made them out to be.

Others may want you to believe the sky is falling because of their insecurity, desire to intentionally or unintentionally assert power over you, or their belief system. It doesn't matter what anyone else thinks. This is the mind and life hack. What you think trumps everything else because it's *your* life.

Decrease the weighting of failure. It may feel like it, but it is not the end of the world. Evolve your thinking to know that rejection or failure is like the rain. Some days it rains, maybe sprinkles or a torrential downpour, and then it stops. After the rain, the sun comes, warms you up, and you may glimpse a rainbow. Neutralize the sting of a hard situation so that it is not a blow. It's an occurrence, one data point in your life. You have the bandwidth to pivot onward.

Problematic People

Dealing with problematic people may require us to use our FON skills. One of the biggest barriers in our lives concerns difficult people, especially those who try to block our progress and achievement. Sometimes we're inclined to be too polite, ignore data-driven evidence, and justify an unsavory character. We may be inclined to:

- Believe that other people are just like us and work hard to earn success.
- Take everyone at face value. The mind and heart want to believe that others are positive and well-intentioned.
- Believe we can change others: *It's different for me. My words and actions will get a better outcome.* In reality, you can't change anyone but yourself.

The CodeBreaker Mindset™ is about using the written and unwritten rules, with informed intuition, to decode people and situations. Develop your pattern recognition on each stakeholder you engage to decipher who is authentic, genuine, transactional, or ill-intentioned.

Archetypes of the People You Will Encounter

Over the span of my career and life, I've learned from brilliant leaders and colleagues to classify people into two broad categories.

1. *Those who want to win.* They don't need to see their name in spotlights or receive recognition. Their mission is not individual success at all costs. They will do whatever it takes and collaborate with others. Their sole objective is the collective win. This person has an abundance mindset.
2. *Those who are afraid to lose.* This person is about me, myself, and I. The individual has to win at all costs and cannot be perceived as not being dominant, the driver, or the winner.

> They will cut off their nose to spoil their face, if necessary. The focus is on that person's agenda of what they equate victory to be, which may have nothing to do with what benefits the team or collective.

The first group is a giver and is others-centered. The second is a taker and is self-centered. Let's take a closer look at some of the personas you may encounter.

The Authentic, Long-Duration Friend or Colleague

Recognize these good people because they are the ones who will partner with you, wish you the best, and stand by you through thick and thin.

The Frenemy

These people are not really your friends. You can't count on them, and they don't substantively support you. On occasion, they will align with you on specific objectives or give the illusion that they are your friend if it somehow serves them.

If they see or perceive other insiders hanging with you, they may warm up to you to give the illusion that the two of you are tight. This is a charade so they can engender more favor with the insiders.

The Saboteur

Saboteurs lurk in the jungles of life, both visible and camouflaged. Depending on their level of power and determination to create chaos and destruction, they will fall into one of the following categories:

- Lightweight saboteur: Their actions tend to be petty, like social exclusion or backstabbing. They may keep you from being on a team or not invite you to a party.

- Medium-weight saboteur: They are focused on self-preservation and are selfish about their own interests. Of less concern to them is how their behavior may hurt you. Their actions may be the best they are capable of to achieve their objectives. That may result in you being roadkill, but that is not their primary *raison d'être.*
- Heavyweight saboteur: Their actions are more vindictive and harmful. They are gunning for you and may do things like try to get you fired. Being calculating on every level is their forte. They are operating using perception- and manipulation-driven information and tactics (see chapter 8).

Scarcity Mindset

Another attribute that motivates the person who doesn't want to lose is living in a scarcity mindset. Saboteurs don't believe there is enough success to go around, so they keep you out of the loop. This often manifests as a blatant lack of acknowledgment.

How to Recognize Saboteurs

When a saboteur pops up, before you can deal with them, you need to decode them. These assassins don't always operate in the open. After an encounter with them, you may be left feeling off, sensing something wasn't quite right. Most of the time, we ignore these feelings or explain them away. Often, the person's behavior is intentional.

Saboteurs make you believe you aren't good enough and block you from opportunities, because they want it for themselves, or they don't want you to benefit from it. These devious actors are playing some level of nth-dimensional chess, using direct or indirect tactics to slow or stop you. Be attentive and learn to assess their motivations so you can then act appropriately.

Saboteur Trademarks

Not Transparent

A saboteur isn't likely to confront you publicly. Their behaviors can be subtle, covert, and passive-aggressive.

Subtle Verbal Attacks

They can make comments, explicit or subtle, that make you believe you aren't good enough in the hopes that diminishing your confidence and self-esteem will cripple you.

Blocks You

One of a saboteur's main weapons is to block you and shut you down. It's always intentional, but not always obvious. They may do it behind the scenes, such as getting someone else to uninvite you to the party or disrupt your activities. Or they may be transparent and attempt this directly.

Interrupt Your High-Stakes Opportunities

"Don't interrupt my money" is what I say to intruders in my conversations, especially when the body language clearly signals "Do not disturb." "Money" is a fun word I use to mean business, productivity, or enjoyment. In a high-stakes room where the attendees are senior and influential, it's an unwritten code to give people space to interact. Unfortunately, not everyone follows this. Some may elbow in to steal their turn.

Maybe the interrupter's intentions are innocent—some are socially awkward and have low EQ. They may or may not be trying to ruin or usurp your moment. Maybe they are curious about what you're talking about and don't want to miss out. Regardless, they're acting as a saboteur, and often, they know exactly what they're doing.

This happened to me on one occasion when I was speaking one-on-one with President Bill Clinton on a matter pertaining to my native land, Guyana. There was a man who'd had his day in the sun with the President but insisted on leaning into my conversation and giving us no peace to speak uninfringed.

How to respond in real time to a situation like this? It is natural and understandable to feel stunned. Paralysis and panic may step in as we try to maintain our cool in front of whoever we are speaking to. We likely feel upset that someone is encroaching on our moment with a very important person. When our emotions flare, it's hard to think clearly.

Have a plan for these actors. If someone does interrupt you, don't choke, get distracted, or get upset. Have a script ready so you can shut down the disruption and keep your cool.

One suggestion would be to say in a tempered voice, "Could you kindly give us a moment? We're just finishing our conversation." This works in both unintentional and intentional sabotage circumstances. Practice this over and over so you are trained. You may not handle the situation well every time, but the more armed you are, the more likely muscle memory will rescue your moment when you are hijacked.

Try not to be shaken. However, if you are, take a breath and reset. Focus on the mission at hand. If you need a pep talk, then internally close your eyes and repeat your recovery mantra, *I am light. I shine. I love myself. I am here to have my conversation. I got this.* You may plant this mantra with a friend and have them text it to you if you lose your way.

Pet to Threat Phenomenon

The pet to threat dilemma is best illustrated in the following workplace scenario. Someone hires and champions you, and at first, is happy to have you on their team. Over time, as you perform well, the same person may become threatened by you. Perhaps you are too competent and effective, and it unintentionally makes others' performances look lackluster. As a result, the boss or your colleagues start treating you differently. This may show up as:

- No longer being "in the know" or the inner circle
- Excluded from key meetings or information
- Ignored or not acknowledged
- Substance not matching the form for your position and authority

(See similar and related identifiers in chapter 4.)

Establish your threshold of how many red flags you experience before deciding to take action. If going from pet to threat is unsustainable or not right for you, you may need to eject yourself. Be assured, at some point, they will sideline you if you don't self-select your exit.

Pretend to Care About You

One of the unsavory character's favorite ways to thwart you is using a well-timed comment or question to knock you off kilter. For example, before an important moment, they lean over and ask, "Are you okay?"

Another phrase is "Are you happy?" This can make you start to question or second-guess yourself, especially if the query comes from a person who is not a trusted stakeholder. Note, we are not talking about those genuine colleagues and friends who are posing questions out of legitimate care. It's odd to me when acquaintances ask, "Are you happy?" because they are not in my life in a substantive way to ask or understand what makes me happy. I am not being cynical. I'm distilling how authenticity can show up. Those who want to know if you are happy when they don't know your story or testimony are often masking nosiness with concern. Think about it, if I told them I'm not happy, would they genuinely offer a helping hand?

Become Self-Conscious

An easy way to become impaired is to have someone comment on your physical appearance or something you just did, which leaves you feeling self-conscious. This can happen in any setting. You'll be engaging in small talk when someone whispers about your clothes or hair. Often, this happens just before you go onstage or take the floor. Timing is everything because a saboteur revels when you are not at your best in the moment that matters. They want you to have little to no time to regroup. CodeBreakers learn to deflect and move on unrattled.

Silent Treatment

Picture this: You're sharing great ideas, and instead of people seeming engaged, they respond like a deer in headlights. They offer no acknowledgment, feedback, or comment. They may say, "Oh, that's not going to work." They don't want to tell you that they don't understand what you're saying, because they don't want to acknowledge that you presented something beyond their intellectual level. This is why they should be hiring you or finding you a place on their team, but they don't because they insist on being the smartest person in the room. The silence is designed to throw you off your game and disable you.

In this scenario, you may consider probing them to gather data-driven observations on what's going on. Ask them, "Do you have any questions on what I said? Was my presentation or communication clear? Do you have any feedback? Can we dialogue on this?" If they say they need to reflect, ask them for a follow-up appointment to discuss. Give them options, and if they take none, then they were not for you—they are the unproductive actor in that scenario. Don't give them any more of your brilliant ideas and energy at that point.

Impostor Treatment vs. Impostor Syndrome

This happens a lot to women, people of color, and frankly, whoever is deemed to be the outsider in the equation. You share an idea, and nobody responds. Blank stares and silence. A few minutes later, someone in the majority or an insider voices the same thought, and they are congratulated. That dynamic is impostor treatment. They are treating you as though you are the impostor and not legitimate. This is a scarcity mindset at work.

You may walk away thinking, "I didn't communicate well," or "My idea was silly and didn't resonate." Especially if you are an outsider, you may internalize and own it as your deficit. This causes you to slink back. No one is born with impostor syndrome. It comes from those who treat us like we are impostors. We then internalize those sentiments that others impose on us and develop impostor syndrome.

Impostor Treatment

There is an ongoing dilemma people face around feeling and experiencing impostor syndrome. It is not impostor syndrome that is the root, but impostor treatment, meaning the phenomenon is not coming from within you, but from those around you. It occurs when others deal with you in a way, either through substance or perception, that signals that they view you as a pretender or not worthy. The opportunity is to catch when you are receiving impostor treatment, block it, and not allow those toxic thoughts to clutch your mind.

Saboteurs Treat You Like an Impostor

Shady actors lob multiple questions to discount your validity. This is designed to create self-doubt in you and those who witness it. These questions may be disguised as interest, but often the person aims to cast suspicion on your legitimacy or minimize your accomplishments. It's not only the content of what is asked, but the tone and implication. Questions may come in the following areas:

- Credentials—Did you really go to that school? Do you have your CPA? (This signals a lack of trust in your qualifications.)
- Experience—Were you really a television journalist? So you worked at Goldman Sachs? What did you do?
- Relationships—Are those your relationships? Or did you inherit them through your company or boss? Do you really know so-and-so? These overtures can be overt or subtle, for example, "Oh, you joined that firm and you picked up those relationships?" (The inference being that the firm already had those relationships and you inherited them.)

It can be tricky to decrypt if stakeholders are intentionally trying to diminish you. If you're not sure, tap your sounding board or trusted comrade and relay the events. They can help you discern. Ask your informed intuition. Often, if it does not feel right, it isn't.

Ndidi Okonkwo Nwuneli, ONE Campaign, President and CEO, spoke about the "burden of proof" in chapter 11. She also says, "We still have a burden of proof as black women in America. I have to prove to people, yes, I deserve to go to Wharton and Harvard. I worked my butt off, graduated with very strong grades. Worked my butt off through all the organizations I've built, which have been profitable, created jobs, changed lives, and still exist today. I deserve a seat at the table. I will come with my full authentic self and be confident to dispel negative narratives, negative stereotypes through the way I live my life and the excellence I bring to everything I do."

Internal Saboteur

We are our own greatest enemy. It is easier to punish ourselves for mistakes than to be gentle and forgiving, like we might be with a loved one.

Being a force of nature means recognizing when we are creating headwinds for ourselves. This may appear as:

- Lack of self-love
- Negative self-talk and self-doubt
- Sabotaging one's own performance, such as being ill-prepared
- Giving up
- Not performing when given the opportunity
- Forgoing the opportunity

Many of us battle negative self-talk daily. Establish the discipline to catch yourself in these moments. Rewire and embrace positive messaging by saying the following affirmations:

I love myself.

I am smart.

I got this.

I am a champion.

I win.

I am victorious.

Chant this at any time. Come up with your own phrases. Be your own hype person.

A Champion of Sports

CASE STUDY

Yannick Colaco, FanCode, Co-Founder, and National Basketball Association (NBA), India, former Managing Director

Yannick Colaco's passion for sports began as a youth athlete. This love traveled to entrepreneurship, where he has dedicated his life to democratizing access to sports, especially for youth, through being the first head of NBA

India, and then co-founding FanCode, India's leading digital sports destination for content and fan merchandise.

Build It and They Will Come

Sports as a part of culture was new to India, despite it being a multi-billion-dollar industry, feeding the appetite of the country's population of almost 1.5 billion fans. Yannick says, "Twenty-five years ago, the concept of sport as part of culture almost didn't exist. Education and how you did in math and science, especially for kids in school, was the priority. Sports were something you did if you had time. It wasn't an important part of the fabric of society. That has changed significantly in the last two decades. It has become part of the culture of schools where every child plays sports. If you walk through any suburb in Mumbai, you will find a lot of turfs where kids are playing football [soccer], basketball, pickleball, or tennis."

Cricket is followed almost like a religion in India, winning the trophy of fandom with the Indian Premier League (IPL) mesmerizing millions of viewers globally. Field hockey, football [soccer], kabaddi, badminton, wrestling, and tennis enjoy significant popularity, with basketball dribbling much lower in the ranking. When Yannick Colaco serendipitously met senior NBA executives, including former Commissioner David Stern, and was recruited to lead NBA India, he jumped at the challenge to popularize basketball and build the NBA's business in the country.

Irrational Optimism

Being a natural competitor, whether as head of NBA India or co-founding FanCode, both ventures were herculean feats, and required Yannick to channel his own FON. Yannick says, "You almost need to have some level of irrational optimism. Let's take basketball as a great example. Every time Stephen Curry [a four-time NBA Champion and one of the greatest players in league history with the Golden State Warriors] shoots, he expects it to go in.

Steph Curry can miss five three-pointers in a row. He will take the sixth shot, expecting it to go in. So, I think there's a level of belief you need to have, a level of adjustment, constantly responding to the information that you have. Most importantly, there is a level of work that is required, especially for new things that have not been developed before. You need to invest hard work in research, relationships, and building [from the] ground up. You need to persevere knowing that what you build may not be what the consumer wants, and you may need to scrap it and build again."

NBA India

Yannick says, "When I joined the NBA in 2013, the goal was always to try and figure out how to grow the game of basketball and with it, the brand of the NBA. Everything was about doing it from the grassroots. That was a vision that then-Commissioner David Stern and, subsequently, Commissioner Adam Silver had been pushing. Commissioner Stern talked about the NBA's destiny in India being directly linked to that of the growth of the game of basketball. He spoke about how the process was important in terms of making basketball popular from the bottom up, getting kids to play, teaching them the right way, building talent, and then that would eventually lead to the growth of the NBA in India."

Partnering with Other Forces of Nature

Leading NBA India, Yannick knew local partners were critical. He says, "Both David Stern and Adam Silver made trips to India to understand the market, people, and nuances." On David Stern's first trip, he met and hit it off with Mukesh Ambani, one of India's most prominent business leaders. He is the patriarch of one of the world's wealthiest billionaire families, and Chairman and largest shareholder of Reliance Industries Limited (RIL), a multi-hundred-billion-dollar diversified conglomerate in areas such as petrochemicals, telecommunications, media, and retail. Yannick says, "Mukesh and Nita Ambani were kind enough to host a dinner at their home for David Stern. He shared his vision of building grassroots basketball. The Ambani family said they were happy to help and partnered with the NBA to launch the Reliance Foundation Junior NBA program.

"The NBA was already a massive global brand and was trying to grow the right way. Taking small steps, it started with the Reliance Foundation Jr. NBA program and then built an academy and basketball schools. It had a licensing program with partners and a media partnership. I helped with launching the first global game in India. All of it was almost a playbook, trying to figure out the right modification for India.

"When we started, no one knew whether this could work. This was about getting physical education teachers to train their students to learn the game of basketball. We started with two cities, and in six years, when I left NBA India, we were in roughly thirty-five cities across the country with nine million kids in the program."

FanCode: A Sports Streaming First

Leading NBA India expanded Yannick's sports ecosystem expertise, and it sparked him to notice a gap in the industry. He says, "Sport fandom in India is over six hundred million fans and growing significantly. However, the economics of linear television and broadcasting meant all stakeholders continued to focus on mass popular sports. The IPL was available on close to fifteen linear channels in different languages and had tremendous marketing and coverage. But La Liga [professional soccer league in Spain] or Bundesliga [professional soccer league in Germany] or domestic cricket didn't have the same amount of coverage. My research revealed that close to 99 percent of professional sports activity in the world didn't have proper coverage, which meant that sports fans didn't have the right access. That's where we saw an opportunity to build a digital platform to address these issues that sports fans face."

FanCode was born out of this labor of love to democratize access and optionality to consuming sports. To recruit the elements to succeed, Yannick sought advice from Harsh Jain, who had co-founded Dream Sports, a successful sports tech company that owns India's leading fantasy sports gaming platform, Dream11. Yannick had known Harsh "for years, and we have a common passion for Manchester United. We're both massive sports fans, speak a similar language, and have done business together. Harsh saw similarities in the engagement model between his own sports businesses and FanCode." The two joined forces, with Dream Sports investing in FanCode to incubate it under India's leading sports technology conglomerate.

Yannick realized, "When you're doing something new, [like] India's first sports-only platform, it was about trying to build quickly and learn. We have this system called 'HEAL,' hypothesis, experimentation, actuals, and learning. Look at the actuals against the hypothesis; modify and consistently correct course to build your product. When something works, how do you double down and grow that quickly? When it doesn't, reassess, make changes, or even drop it. You have the ability to get consumer feedback quickly.

"Everything starts with consumer need. The sports business is different from everything else. There is an over-indexation on passion. I don't think anything incites the level of tribalism or passion that sports does among fans, and that's to be harnessed. It's also a big challenge because you can't afford to make mistakes. You can't have a single second of dropped content on a live game because that same passion then goes away from the sports fan towards the technology provider.

"Sports as a form of entertainment is pure in that the story that you're watching as a consumer is actually being written as you watch. No one knows what's going to happen when you're watching a movie on Netflix or your favorite streamer. It's a drama or comedy with a cast of characters. The story is already written, and you are watching it. A live sports game is unique in that once the game is over and recorded, the nature of that entertainment changes. It's also something we look to channel as the live element of sports is what binds communities and fans together."

The first-of-its-kind sports streaming platform in India has surpassed expectations in its six years of operation. Yannick beams as he shares that FanCode has scaled to "over one hundred and sixty million users, streaming close to twenty thousand live games a year across twelve different sports. We are extremely excited by the business that we are building."

On tapping that FON within to punch through, especially when battling the naysayers, Yannick says, "It's the people around you that you trust: family, friends, mentors, who believe in you. It's people who trust that you will do the right thing. It's every fan, every single person who works with FanCode. It's their trust that fuels."

Be Victorious

There are mean people and bullies everywhere. Part of our hesitation in owning our FON comes from worrying about what others think. Who cares? They are not paying our rent nor putting food on our table. One of the biggest self-realization opportunities is to neutralize and erase the negative impact others have on us. That is being a force of nature in and of itself.

Hustler

Why do we brand people, especially outsiders, as aggressive? Is it not okay for them to hustle for themselves? To take their shot, go up to the leader, and ask for the meeting? We hate on go-getters because they are doing what we can't or won't do. To make ourselves feel good, we put the other person down and label them as forceful. Jealous of their hustle, we lash out with verbal attacks to slow them down or lure them off track.

You'll always have dissenters. Remember, dogs don't bark at parked cars (see chapter 11). No one is paying attention to you if your work is inconsequential.

Being a force of nature is fortifying your mind, body, soul, and spirit to wake up every day, living in your creation, and championing for yourself, for others, and your dreams.

Remember, there are more than eight billion people on the planet. Not everyone will like you or do business with you. Focus on finding those you have alignment with.

Make it happen! You already are by reading these pages. The force of nature has lived inside of you from the moment of your birth. Let it ignite and power your CodeBreaker Mindset™!

The CodeBreaker Mindset™ Takeaways

- Everyone is born with some force of nature within. Embrace, nurture, and act on it.
- Wear your resilience like a badge of honor. Cultivate and continuously strengthen your resilience muscle.
- Equip your pattern recognition with the artillery to detect and decode saboteurs and those who perpetrate you with impostor treatment. Neutralize and outmaneuver them.

Chapter 14

Cultivating The CodeBreaker Mindset™

> These fragments I have shored against my ruins.[70]
>
> —T.S. Eliot, poet, playwright, and
> Nobel Prize in Literature recipient

This quote from T.S. Eliot's poem "The Waste Land" is a way of describing the importance of gathering up the fragments of meaning to build a barrier against the growing sense of chaos. When we pull together our wisdom, we can bring stability to what feels broken.

In a very real sense, The CodeBreaker Mindset™ is my contribution to shoring up the experiences I've had in business and life—whether from observing human behavior, analyzing the landscape of competitive forces, or learning through the school of hard knocks.

Despite enduring personal and professional challenges, seriously wondering at times if I was going to make it, I've shifted to a space of wanting to create again. I knew from a young age that my life purpose would be to help people. That calling is stronger now than ever. I call it living in creation. We are given life not to just exist, but to create our best selves in order to give our best for positive outcomes.

My hope is that the fragments I'm offering will help make your road a little less rocky and will encourage you to keep going. When you know that you are valuable and have valuable things to offer, you can shift from enduring to living abundantly and help others do the same.

As I've tried to emphasize while journeying through *The CodeBreaker Mindset*™ together, it takes collective wisdom to achieve the greatest heights. I am grateful to have interviewed leaders from the highest echelon of diverse industries and parts of the world. These leaders shared their brilliant take on cultivating The CodeBreaker Mindset™. May their responses guide you toward achieving your dreams and pursuits, and living your best life, as they have for me.

Let their words inspire and energize you to act!

Leaders' Takes on *The CodeBreaker Mindset*™

Tory Burch, Tory Burch LLC, Founder, Executive Chairman, Chief Creative Officer

"Embrace change, and never let anyone put you in a box."

Navin Chaddha, Mayfield Fund, Managing Partner

Be yourself, take the leap, and go.

"When you go to school, everybody takes a common exam. In life, everyone gets a different exam. So figure out the strategy of you, the value of you, and personalize it; don't get into analysis paralysis. Just be yourself; be authentic.

"Follow your dream and don't think about the downside. Fear is the only thing that limits your potential. So get that out of your system. The worst that can happen is you'll fail. Einstein said, 'If you're never failed, you're not going to come up with anything new.'

"What's your vision? What are your values? Once you figure that out, jump in. Be bold; success will follow. One door will open other doors. Be yourself, take the leap, and go. That's the mindset. If I can tell anyone anything, it's have that."

Kazembe Ajamu, 5Tre The Blade, Founder and CEO, and Father of Zendaya

There is a code to be cracked.

"It's like a puzzle with stepping stones that lead you to certain destinations in your life. Our lives take several paths at the same time. So once you crack the code on one thing, that tells you there was a code to be cracked. Then you crack the code on another thing. And once you start, it's like a video game where, after you make it to a certain stage, you get rewarded, you get extra points. That's the way I see The CodeBreaker Mindset™. As you break the codes, different windows of life open up for you.

"My advice on how to cultivate The CodeBreaker Mindset™ is to get out of your own way! Most people, no matter what profession, are ignorant. I don't mean stupid ignorant. I mean they just don't know what they don't know. If you give a six-month-old baby a 20-carat diamond to play with, that diamond means nothing to that child, but it means something to somebody else because they understand the value. The baby has extreme naivete. Some people lack exposure, lack knowledge. If I don't know I'm supposed to only work eight hours a day, and you give me a job and work me sixteen hours a day, I think this is just the way it goes. So you have to become aware enough to realize that you are ignorant of what you don't know."

Bruce Cohen, Academy and Tony Award–winning and Emmy-Nominated Producer

Stick the landing.

"In many cases, the codes you're trying to break are other human beings. Whatever your goal is, professionally or personally, most of the time, it's other people who are between you and your goal. So, to me, The Code-Breaker Mindset™ is understanding who you are, understanding the person you're speaking to, using every cue at your disposal to figure out how you want the conversation to go, what you want to bring up, when you want to bring it up, how you want to bring it up, and then trying to make that happen.

"In every phone call, in every email, in every conversation, you're trying to stick the landing. If you think too hard about that, (a) you'll drive yourself crazy, and (b) there's probably just not enough bandwidth in the human brain. It has to come naturally. That's another skill to The CodeBreaker Mindset™: Know how you want to break the code and why, and then work to make it more intuitive. That's when you'll start sticking landings left, right, and center because that'll be a skill you developed and now comes naturally to you."

Yannick Colaco, FanCode, Co-Founder, and NBA, India, former Managing Director

Be present.

"Be fully present. This is not just professionally. I learn this for myself in everything I do, whether it is spending time with kids and friends. You always have thoughts in your mind. I struggled when I was with someone to be fully present. I think being present takes a lot of practice. That helps me be more impactful in terms of everything that I have, personal and professional relationships.

"It's about the mindset where you are in that moment, where you are in that particular phase of your life and time. Use all your past experiences, the information that you have from the past that you have already assimilated, and be able to react to situations in front of you. Don't get too obsessed with looking in front of you five or six years out because no one knows, right? For professionals, don't get too consumed by what you are going to be one, three, or five years from now."

Mindy Grossman, Consello, Partner and Vice Chair; Fanatics, Board Member; former CEO of WW

Push yourself into discomfort zones.

"I think it's about the analytical and visionary. It's about what your personal strategy is for success. It's about being able to use risk-taking and boldness as the essence of transformations. It's the ability to really push yourself into what I call discomfort zones, but at the end of the day, to see not just what's in front of you, but to see what could be. To me, that's what CodeBreaking must do.

"My advice on how to cultivate The CodeBreaker Mindset™ goes back to knowing enough to ask the right questions about everything. It's about having the curiosity. It's about putting yourself into situations where you're not entirely comfortable and being able to look for what's not there yet, and surrounding yourself and building relationships with people who are like that as well."

Jon Korngold, Blackstone, Global Head of Blackstone Growth

You've got just one you.

"There's so much serendipity in life. How can you become agile and take advantage of opportunities in a way that's authentic to yourself? You've got just one you; you've got one reputation. Use that as your true north, no matter what the world is dealing you, and maintain who you are, headwinds or tailwinds. Never compromise your integrity or your morals. If you do that right, good things generally happen.

"The CodeBreaker Mindset™ is recognizing that most of what's around you is not in your control. All you can control are your core principles. If you surround yourself with great friends, they'll look out for you and make sure you stay out of trouble.

"The CodeBreaker Mindset™ is asking, 'How do I draw from all that is great around me, recognizing so much is not in my control?' If you harness that right, you can do some amazing things and ultimately bet on yourself. And hopefully you're in the right environment where people will support you becoming the best version of yourself."

Steve Kraus, Bessemer Venture Partners, Partner

Every human being has some unique angle they bring to the world, so explore what is yours.

"CodeBreaker means you're doing something different, unusual, challenging the status quo, disruptive, innovative, whatever you want to. The mindset part means doing what's really hard because you have a unique edge or you're a force of nature. You have to be constantly learning. You have to be willing to be okay with failing, but learning from the failures. In order to break the code, you need strong mental fortitude and flexible thinking because there will be lots of headwinds, and you're trying to thread the needle in the middle of the storm and make it all happen. It also takes some luck. You have to realize that a lot of entrepreneurs fail the first time and second time. Entrepreneurs are really interesting because they learn from their failures. They iterate and then, eventually, luck comes their way.

"Make investments in yourself. Every human being has some unique angle that they bring to the world, so explore what yours is."

Ndidi Okonkwo Nwuneli, ONE Campaign, President and CEO

Be humble, hungry, and have courage.

"The term CodeBreaker means going against the grain and against the norm. To challenge the status quo and live an impactful life by the way you tackle problems, take on opportunities, and deliver impact. Where you feel like oftentimes people are excluded from contexts because of the written rules, you can break through because you've come with your own set of rules or found a way to navigate with your own attributes, talents, and creativity.

"Mindset is how we think about the world. For me, I find it helpful to have a growth mindset, a mindset that believes in the possible, a mindset that sees opportunities where other people see problems, a mindset that embraces risk-taking, but also embraces faith.

"So, combining both CodeBreaker and mindset means having an attitude to life that is brimming with possibilities, that allows individuals who want to be leaders to take on difficult tasks and make an impact because of how they think, how they live, and what approaches they utilize.

"My advice on how to cultivate The CodeBreaker Mindset™ is three things. These are the same three I use to attract mission-driven high achievers. Every individual who wants to be a CodeBreaker should be humble, hungry, and have courage. For me, the biggest barrier we have today with many young people is this humility piece. This life is a journey. Stretch yourself to learn and unlearn and, every day, commit to having the courage, the humility, and the wisdom to do hard things because it matters, because you matter, and because the world is waiting."

Ken Ohashi, Brooks Brothers, CEO

Figure out who the decision maker is in the room and how you get there.

"There are moments of really understanding yourself. I push my teams to be introspective thinkers. Philosophically, I always want to get to the right answer. I don't care if I'm right or wrong. Having that mindset will shortcut a lot of noise along the way because people can really get mired into process and politics and people dynamics. But ultimately, if you can see the North Star clearly, and you can get there faster, you will cut out a lot of that noise. Also, the nuance is to understand which relationships will get you there faster and then to cultivate those relationships.

"I was doing business in China once, and someone said, 'Who's the decision maker in the room?' because so many people were in the room. Ultimately, there's always a decision maker in the room. That's the person who can lift you. Figuring out who that is and how you get there is, again, about getting to the right answer and not having to be right. That person is paving the way for the right answer, so quickly understanding that is key."

Michelle Peluso, Revlon, CEO and Nike, Board Member

Future-proof your career and company.

"I think it's so easy to get caught up in the day-to-day. And then I went home and I have the kids, husband, the board that I'm on, the community that I'm doing and checking in with my family and friends. I think the question becomes, how do you make sure you're cultivating the time, the network, and the reading? Whatever it takes to put yourself in the space of the future, to put yourself in the space of being a disruptor.

"That can happen in the meetings you're in every day. Just taking some space to ask the question, how might we be wrong? How might technology fundamentally change the way we perceive supply chain? Or forward loading inventory? Or maybe in bigger moments where you cultivate a few hours out of the day job to bring a futurist in or to bring somebody who thinks about the world really differently, to talk to you and the team.

"I do think it's the mindset. It's the time and it's the kind of network and learning that helps you make sure you're always future-proofing your own career, your own company."

Reshma Saujani, Girls Who Code and Moms First, Founder

Just do it!

"Number one, you just do it. Sometimes we make the thing so big that it scares us off. Number two, you have to be disciplined. With my company, Girls Who Code, I built one product, and I built it well. Once that product was sailing, I built the next one. Same thing at Moms First. We could have been working on so many things, but we decided to get really focused and disciplined on the issues, on the messaging, and on what we were trying to create."

Dr. Astro Teller, The Moonshot Factory (division of Alphabet), Co-Founder and Captain

Play the long game.

"Decide what you believe, then work backwards from the end. There are a lot of things, the habits that we work on at X (The Moonshot Factory), it's still hard, and I won't say that we're doing it perfectly at getting everyone here to practice them. But what I can say is, I have zero doubt that playing the long game is what we should be doing. And every time, in every way, where I find us not doing that, I say, 'Nope.' How will we instill that in our culture in a workable way? I'm not exactly sure. But at no point do I say, 'Yeah, all right, forget playing the long game.' So I would encourage everyone to pick that set of things they believe in, start with the end in mind, and then work backwards on how to design a set of habits that will reliably get them there."

Dr. David Thomas, Morehouse College, President

Be consumed with trying to create the experience of yourself that you want to have in the world.

"First, don't be consumed with seeking the brass ring. Be consumed with trying to create the experience of yourself that you want to have in the world. Some of us seek things, others of us simply seek an experience. Oftentimes, if you're able to seek an experience, you'll make decisions that don't make sense to other people.

"So try to figure out what's the experience you really want to have in the world and go for that. Oftentimes, it won't make sense to other people. But as long as it's making sense to you, you'll do well there.

"Second, learn to be comfortable with yourself in situations that are not designed for you. That's how you actually become powerful as an individual, transcendent of what your title is. When I was at Wharton, there were only two other black professors at the school. My white colleagues would often comment about how comfortable I seemed in that environment. And it was cutthroat. It was brutal for young faculty members.

"But what they were really shocked by was realizing, 'Hey, you're a black guy, and you seem more comfortable than us white guys. You sit in meetings; you say things that everybody else is thinking but won't say.' I'm just comfortable with who I am. Anywhere I go, I figure I belong.

"So I tell my protégés, in particular the black ones, not to buy into the notion of impostor syndrome. I think it's a racist ploy to undermine the confidence of minorities and women in predominantly white and male organizations and in roles that potentially can lead them to have real power. If you're in a room, you're supposed to be there. You're not an impostor. You have to figure out how to be there, not be worried about whether you belong or whether you're posing. We all love a label that tells us we're normal when we feel abnormal."

BD Wong, Tony Award–winning and Emmy-Nominated Actor

Be open.

"Without even knowing it, I live by The CodeBreaker Mindset™. I don't see things at face value. I'll often see a relationship or an introduction, like the way I met you, as a kind of introduction to something that I don't know quite what it is, but it feels positive. I think, *Wait, what is the possibility of this?* I meet people all the time, and I've learned and grown to love being open to things.

"You can't go through the day without encountering something that can open a door for you. I don't mean open a door of opportunity, necessarily. I mean open a door to knowledge or insight or a relationship you didn't expect. I'm glad you're encouraging people to be open to that, to look forward to every opportunity, and to embrace it.

"I get invited to do a number of things for a number of reasons. Most of the time, I will leave afterward and think, I didn't really want to do that, but it turned out well. I met some great people. I knew I would. I just had to be open to it."

I hope the advice from these leaders embracing The CodeBreaker Mindset™ motivates and empowers you to value and victory in all aspects of your life.

Acknowledgments

I am grateful to the following leaders for their invaluable insights and support:

Tory Burch, Tory Burch LLC, Founder, Executive Chairman, Chief Creative Officer

Navin Chaddha, Mayfield Fund, Managing Partner

Kazembe Ajamu, 5Tre The Blade, Founder and CEO, and Father of Zendaya

Bruce Cohen, Academy and Tony Award–winning and Emmy-Nominated Producer

Yannick Colaco, FanCode, Co-Founder, and NBA, India, former Managing Director

Mindy Grossman, Consello, Partner and Vice Chair; Fanatics, Board Member; and former CEO of WW

Jon Korngold, Blackstone, Global Head of Blackstone Growth

Steve Kraus, Bessemer Venture Partners, Partner

Ken Ohashi, Brooks Brothers, CEO

Ndidi Okonkwo Nwuneli, ONE Campaign, President and CEO

Michelle Peluso, Revlon, CEO, and Nike, Board Member

Reshma Saujani, Girls Who Code and Moms First, Founder

Dr. Astro Teller, The Moonshot Factory (division of Alphabet), Co-Founder and Captain

Dr. David Thomas, Morehouse College, President

BD Wong, Tony Award–winning and Emmy-Nominated Actor

Dean Srikant Datar, Harvard Business School

Professor Linda Hill, Harvard Business School

Professor Rajiv Lal, Harvard Business School

Neil Foote

Thasunda Brown Duckett, TIAA, President & CEO; Nike, Board Member; and NY Liberty, Investor

Sarah Friar, OpenAI, Chief Financial Officer, and Walmart, Board Member

Frank McKenna, C.M., TD Bank Group, Vice Chairman; former Ambassador of Canada to the United States; and former Premier of New Brunswick

Thomas S. Caldwell, C.M., Caldwell Financial Ltd. & Urbana Corporation, Chairman

Sanjiv Mehta, *L* Catterton India, Executive Chairman, and Hindustan Unilever, former Chairman and CEO

VN "Tiger" Tyagarajan, Bain Capital, Senior Advisor; BCG, Senior Advisor; Jabil Inc., Board Member; Kantar, Board Member; and Genpact, former President and CEO

James White, The Honest Company, Chairman of the Board, and Jamba Inc., former Chairman, President & CEO

Notes

1. Pliny the Elder, *Natural History*, 2.5.
2. "What Does Friendship Look Like in America?" Pew Research Center, accessed December 2024. https://www.pewresearch.org/short-reads/2023/10/12/what-does-friendship-look-like-in-america/.
3. X, The Moonshot Factory, "Homepage," accessed December 2024. https://x.company.
4. Chuck Palahniuk, *Lullaby* (Vintage/Random House, 2003).
5. Merriam-Webster.com Dictionary, "suspend (one's) disbelief," accessed November 6, 2024. https://www.merriam-webster.com/dictionary/suspend%20%28one%27s%29%20disbelief.
6. Widely attributed to Rumi, this popular saying appears in various modern collections and popular spiritual texts.
7. "Slavery Abolition Act, [United Kingdom 1883]," Britannica, accessed January 2025. https://www.britannica.com/topic/Slavery-Abolition-Act; "Indian Labour in British Guiana," History Today, accessed January 2025. https://www.historytoday.com/archive/indian-labour-british-guiana.
8. Michael Adas, "A New System of Slavery: The Export of Indian Labour Overseas, 1830–1920. By Hugh Tinker. London: Oxford University Press, 1974. Pp. Xvi, 432 + 18 Plates. £5.75," *The Journal of Economic History*

34, no. 4 (1974): 1062–63. https://doi.org/10.1017/S0022050700089695; Michael Mahoney, "A 'new system of slavery'? The British West Indies and the origins of Indian indenture," *The National Archives Blog*, December 3, 2020, archived at https://blog.nationalarchives.gov.uk/a-new-system-of-slavery-the-british-west-indies-and-the-origins-of-indian-indenture/.

9. "The lost city of gold was thought to be in the mountains of present-day Guyana. The city of gold was referred to as El Dorado." "Sir Walter Raleigh and His First Journey to El Dorado," Thought.co, accessed January 2025. https://www.thoughtco.com/walter-raleighs-journey-to-el-dorado-2136440.
10. Ralph Waldo Emerson, "Plato; or, the Philosopher," in *Representative Men* (1850).
11. Will Smith, interview, *Impact Theory*, YouTube.
12. Image from "Normal Distribution: What It Is, Uses, and Formula," Investopedia. https://www.investopedia.com/terms/n/normaldistribution.asp#:~:text=The%20Bottom%20Line-,Normal%20distribution%2C%20also%20known%20as%20the%20Gaussian%20distribution%2C%20is%20a,defined%20by%20the%20standard%20deviation.
13. "Social Media and News Fact Sheet," Pew Research Center, accessed December 2024. https://www.pewresearch.org/journalism/fact-sheet/social-media-and-news-fact-sheet/.
14. "Users say they regularly encounter false and misleading content on social media—but also new ideas," Pew Research Center, accessed December 2024. https://www.pewresearch.org/internet/2019/05/13/users-say-they-regularly-encounter-false-and-misleading-content-on-social-media-but-also-new-ideas/.
15. "The social media context interferes with truth discernment," Science Advances, accessed December 2024. https://www.science.org/doi/10.1126/sciadv.abo6169
16. Popularly attributed to Pablo Picasso.
17. Harvard Business School home page, accessed December 2024. https://www.hbs.edu/.
18. Stanford Graduate School of Business home page, accessed December 2024. https://www.gsb.stanford.edu/.

19. *Forbes* profile, accessed January 2025. https://www.forbes.com/profile/navin-chaddha/
20. 15 percent of a child actor's gross earnings is required to be placed in a Cooogan Trust per the Jackie Coogan Law. Source: California Family Code § 6752, enacted as part of the California Child Actor's Bill, popularly known as the Jackie Coogan Law.
21. Muhammad Ali, *The Greatest: My Own Story* (1975).
22. CO by U.S. Chamber of Commerce, accessed December 2024. https://www.uschamber.com/co/good-company/growth-studio/successful-companies-that-reinvented-their-business.
23. Maya Angelou, *The Oprah Winfrey Show*, 1986.
24. Deepak Chopra, *Synchrodestiny: Harnessing the Infinite Power of Coincidence to Create Miracles* (Pimlico, 2005).
25. "Serendipity." *Merriam-Webster's Unabridged Dictionary*, Merriam-Webster. https://unabridged.merriam-webster.com/unabridged/serendipity. Accessed December 27, 2024.
26. "Mackay: Successful people from business leaders to athletes use visualization to improve," *Minnesota Star Tribune*, accessed December 2024. https://www.startribune.com/mackay-successful-people-from-business-leaders-to-athletes-use-visualization-to-improve/600332997.
27. "Intuition: What It Is and How It Works," *Psychology Today*, accessed December 2024. https://www.psychologytoday.com/intl/blog/explorations-of-the-mind/202308/intuition-what-it-is-and-how-it-works#:~:text=There%20is%20growing%20evidence%20suggesting,may%20get%20better%20at%20it.
28. Ibid.
29. Ibid.
30. "What motivates children to start walking?" Stack Exchange, Biology, accessed December 2024. https://biology.stackexchange.com/questions/96034/what-motivates-children-to-start-walking.
31. Roy Harrod, *The Life of John Maynard Keynes* (1951).
32. "Triangulation." *Merriam-Webster's Unabridged Dictionary*, Merriam-Webster. https://unabridged.merriam-webster.com/unabridged/triangulation. Accessed January 29, 2025.

33. Theodore Roosevelt, "Citizenship in a Republic," Speech at the Sorbonne, Paris, April 23, 1910.
34. "Private Equity Explained with Examples and Ways to Invest," Investopedia, accessed January 2025. https://www.investopedia.com/terms/p/privateequity.asp.
35. "Private Equity vs. Venture Capital: What's the Difference?" Investopedia, accessed January 2025. https://www.investopedia.com/ask/answers/020415/what-difference-between-private-equity-and-venture-capital.asp.
36. "Remarks at the University of Kansas, March 18, 1968, Robert F. Kennedy, University of Kansas, March 18, 1968. John F. Kennedy Presidential Library and Museum," accessed February 2025. https://www.jfklibrary.org/learn/about-jfk/the-kennedy-family/robert-f-kennedy/robert-f-kennedy-speeches/remarks-at-the-university-of-kansas-march-18 1968#:~:text=I%20think%20there's%20more%20that,Kennedy%20Presidential%20Library.
37. Chuck Palahniuk, *Lullaby* (Vintage/Random House, 2003).
38. "How a small but vocal minority of social media users distort reality and sow division," PBS News, accessed December 2024. https://www.pbs.org/newshour/show/how-a-small-but-vocal-minority-of-social-media-users-distort-reality-and-sow-division.
39. "Nearly a Third of U.S. Professionals Are Career Sleepwalking: A Career Pivot Could Be Your Wake Up Call," LinkedIn official blog, accessed January 2025. https://www.linkedin.com/blog/member/career/nearly-a-third-of-us-professionals-are-career-sleepwalking-career-pivot.
40. "U.S. Adults Prefer Playing It Safe Rather Than Taking Risks with Their Money, Careers and Social Lives," PR Newswire, accessed January 2025. https://www.prnewswire.com/news-releases/us-adults-prefer-playing-it-safe-rather-than-taking-risks-with-their-money-careers-and-social-lives-300972273.html.
41. "Risk Aversion—Everything You Need to Know," InsideBE, accessed February 2025. https://insidebe.com/articles/risk-aversion/.
42. Ibid.
43. Ibid.
44. Ibid.

45. "Career Sleepwalkers: Who They Are And How to Wake Them Up," *Forbes*, accessed January 2025. https://www.forbes.com/sites/joshbersin/2018/08/15/career-sleepwalkers-who-they-are-and-how-to-wake-them-up/.
46. Virgil, *Aeneid*.
47. Poem based on a composition by Kent Keith but Mother Teresa revised and spiritualized it. Prayer Foundation, accessed January 2025. https://prayerfoundation.net/st-teresa-of-calcutta-mother-teresa-do-it-anyway/.
48. Ray Dalio, *Principles: Life and Work*.
49. "Understanding the Law of Attraction," Very Well Mind, accessed January 2025. https://www.verywellmind.com/understanding-and-using-the-law-of-attraction-3144808#:~:text=The%20law%20of%20attraction%20is,health%2C%20finances%2C%20and%20relationships.
50. "Positive Self Talk for Your Athletes," CoachesToolbox.net, accessed January 2025. https://www.coachestoolbox.net/mental-toughness/positive-self-talk-for-your-athletes.
51. "What We Do, the Issues," One, accessed January 2025. https://www.one.org/what-we-do/the-issues/.
52. "Leaving the Crab Bucket Behind," LinkedIn, accessed January 2025. https://www.linkedin.com/pulse/leaving-crab-bucket-behind-escaping-mentality-holding-bise--pvsje/.
53. Malcolm Gladwell, *Outliers: The Story of Success*.
54. "Outlier." *Merriam-Webster's Collegiate Dictionary*, Merriam-Webster, https://unabridged.merriam-webster.com/collegiate/outlier. Accessed January 7, 2025.
55. Ibid.
56. "Then and Now: A History of Social Networking Sites," CBS News, accessed January 2025. https://www.cbsnews.com/pictures/then-and-now-a-history-of-social-networking-sites/.
57. "How Justin Bieber proved that YouTube can produce pop stars," CBC, accessed January 2025. https://www.cbc.ca/music/how-justin-bieber-proved-that-youtube-can-produce-pop-stars-1.5163197.
58. Ibid.
59. "Justin Bieber," Biography, accessed January 2025. https://www.biography.com/musicians/justin-bieber.

60. "How Justin Bieber proved that YouTube can produce pop stars," CBC, accessed January 2025. https://www.cbc.ca/music/how-justin-bieber-proved-that-youtube-can-produce-pop-stars-1.5163197.
61. "Justin Bieber," *Billboard*, accessed January 2025. https://www.billboard.com/artist/justin-bieber/#:~:text=Bieber%20released%20his%20first%20EP,16%20on%20the%20Hot%20100.
62. "Justin Bieber," Wikipedia, accessed January 2025. https://en.wikipedia.org/wiki/Justin_Bieber#:~:text=Bieber%20is%20one%20of%20the,over%20150%20million%20records%20worldwide.
63. "How Justin Bieber proved that YouTube can produce pop stars," CBC, accessed January 2025. https://www.cbc.ca/music/how-justin-bieber-proved-that-youtube-can-produce-pop-stars-1.5163197.
64. "Galileo," Britannica, accessed January 2025. https://www.britannica.com/biography/Galileo-Galilei.
65. "Preparations for Next Moonwalk Simulations Underway (and Underwater)," Explore, accessed February 2025. https://science.nasa.gov/solar-system/galileos-observations-of-the-moon-jupiter-venus-and-the-sun/.
66. Ptolemy (died c. 170 CE) was an Egyptian astronomer, mathematician, and geographer whose writings represent the culminating achievement of Greco-Roman science, particularly his geocentric model of the universe now known as the Ptolemaic system. https://www.britannica.com/science/geocentric-model.
67. "Galileo goes on trial for heresy," History, accessed January 2025. https://www.history.com/this-day-in-history/galileo-is-accused-of-heresy.
68. "The Rise of the Social Media Influencer," PLNU Viewpoint, accessed January 2025. https://viewpoint.pointloma.edu/the-rise-of-the-social-media-influencer/.
69. Deion Sanders, *The Tamron Hall Show.*
70. T.S. Eliot, *The Waste Land.*

About the Author

Chitra Nawbatt's CodeBreaker Mindset™ Journey

Chitra Nawbatt is a unique multi-industry and multidisciplinary executive, recognized for her extensive expertise as a business launcher and builder, growth operator, investor, and media creator.

As a first-generation university graduate, from humble beginnings in South America, Chitra's impressive CodeBreaker Mindset™ journey pierced barriers and ceilings across more than six highly coveted global industries. She was one of the youngest recruited to global professional services firm EY while still an undergraduate student. Chitra emerged as an early adopter and innovator in fintech. At Deutsche Bank, in addition to achieving C-Suite roles, she created working capital fintech and analytics software, well before fintech became an industry category.

Chitra then defied career gravity making a nonlinear pivot, becoming a TV news anchor in New York City, the #1 media market in the world, for Reuters, BNN Bloomberg, CCTV, and other reputable media networks. Her live broadcasts were seen by millions around the world, where her reporting focused on companies, markets, and consumers globally. She conducted exclusive domain-driven and in-depth interviews with global leaders such as the Citigroup CEO, Governor of the Bank of England, and World Boxing Council Heavyweight Champion.

In her next adventure, Chitra aligned her passion and expertise as a business launcher and builder by becoming a partner at General Catalyst, a leading multi-billion-dollar global venture capital firm. As the Global Head of Health Assurance and Innovation, Chitra led the expansion and execution of the firm's Health Assurance ecosystem investment strategy. She also developed and executed new investment theses at the intersections of technology, media, fintech, and consumer. Unique to the venture capital industry, Chitra created and led an inaugural value creation and ecosystem business development function. She originated, commercialized, and managed strategic innovation partnerships for General Catalyst, more than seventy-five of its portfolio companies, and stakeholders, delivering network effect, go-to-market, and revenue acceleration.

As a strategic growth operator, Chitra has held leadership roles in various technology, consulting and early stage companies, pioneering a new category of function as Market Maker, with the unique distinction of being industry-agnostic in scope. In these roles she delivered artificial intelligence, digital transformation, and analytics solutions to Fortune 500 C-Suite executives.

Chitra is the author and host of *The CodeBreaker Mindset*™ book and podcast. The book provides a professional judgment and decision-making framework for accelerating business growth, leadership, and career pivots. The podcast is where leaders share their pursuit journeys to life opportunities, business building, and value creation, as well as the rules, pivots, and serendipity that propel them forward. Chitra has created several other media properties, including podcasts, where she interviewed C-level leaders, entrepreneurs, and investors on growth, innovation, business building, and investing.

Chitra has been involved in various philanthropic activities such as serving on the President of the United States Advance Team (The White House), and as an Adjunct Professor at Rutgers Business School. Her passions include mentoring students and global entrepreneurs; music, having studied and played several instruments; and speaking French.

Chitra has a Certified Public Accountant (CPA) designation, and is a graduate of Harvard Business School, Harvard University, and Rotman School of Management, University of Toronto.